Praise for *Hope Always*

"Leaning on the insights of the saints, teachings of the Church, wisdom from the Bible, and stories from years of ministry, *Hope Always* provides our youth and young adults with a resource that has the potential to inspire them not to give up on God in their walk toward eternity."

Fr. Joshua Johnson, priest of the Diocese of Baton Rouge, author, podcast host of *Ask Fr. Josh*

"Kris does a masterful job of not only explaining what hope is, but also helping us to understand how to cling to, long for, and live in it. With all that we face in the world today, and with despair lingering in many hearts, this book is essential reading for anyone who longs to see the light and grow in the virtue of hope."

Katie Prejean McGrady, international speaker and author

"We need hope now more than ever. It's easy to be discouraged and anxious. Whether because of a repeat sin or wrestling with doubt, sometimes we feel like giving up. Kris Frank has written a book filled with hope! You are not alone. There are amazing saints who have struggled just like you! This book is a great encouragement to any who could use a reminder that all is not lost. I love these words and know that many will be blessed by this book!"

Chris Padgett, speaker, musician, author,
YouTuber at *Happy Place Homestead*,
www.chrispadgett.com

"The virtue of hope can be overwhelming and hard to understand. That's true for everyone, but especially for our modern-day youth and young adults who have been fed lies of relativism and hopelessness from every angle. Kris has experience working with a population that doesn't always have hope so obviously present to them. He also has a passion to help people—as evidenced by his national speaking reputation and youth ministry. His experience and his faith have inspired him to write this delightful book, filled with Scripture, spirituality, theology, and real-life application, which make the theological virtue of hope more accessible, understandable, and practical. *Hope Always* is a wonderful read and an invitation you can't refuse!"

Fr. Leo E. Patalinghug, IVDei, TV and radio host, author,
speaker, founder of www.PlatingGrace.com
and www.TheTableFoundation.org

"No matter where we come from, no one gets through life unscathed. Kris Frank has given us a personal and compelling book that engages life head-on with wisdom to face all its trials, doubts, and disappointments. As Kris says, "Christian hope never disappoints"—through testimony, stories, and Scripture, this book unpacks why and how Jesus Christ is our true anchor and hope. A must-read and an inspiring book that will accompany countless people as they navigate this life!"

Sarah Swafford, speaker and author of *Emotional Virtue:*
A Guide to Drama-Free Relationships

"This little book is a big deal. Kris Frank pulls from 2,000 years of Catholic tradition as well as from his personal experiences as a youth minister, evangelizer, husband, and father in order to introduce (or reintroduce) his readers to the theological virtue of hope. His reflections on doubt and anxiety are particularly excellent and most timely. It's the right book for today's world."

Fr. Damian Ference, priest of the Diocese of Cleveland,
author of *The Strangeness of Truth*

"'Life's great sufferings put other sufferings in perspective,' so writes Kris Frank in this wonderful book. Guided by the saints and Sacred Scripture and dramatically enhanced by powerful personal stories, Frank guides us on our own rediscovery of hope. Offering counsel amid discouragement, suffering, and despair, this book is sure to become a life raft for many to weather the storms of life with peace and joy!"

Andrew Swafford, STD, associate professor
of Theology, Benedictine College; author and host
of *Romans: The Gospel of Salvation*

HOPE ALWAYS

OUR ANCHOR IN LIFE'S STORMS

By Kris Frank

Pauline
BOOKS & MEDIA
Boston

Library of Congress Control Number: 2020930116
CIP data is available.

ISBN 10: 0-8198-3463-7
ISBN 13: 978-0-8198-3463-8

Many manufacturers and sellers distinguish their products through the use of trademarks. Any trademarked designations that appear in this book are used in good faith but are not authorized by, associated with, or sponsored by the trademark owners.

Every effort has been made to trace copyright holders and to obtain their permission for the use of copyright material. The publisher apologizes for any errors or omissions in the list below and would be grateful if notified of any corrections that should be incorporated in future reprints or editions of this book.

Scripture texts in this work are taken from the *New American Bible, Revised Edition,* © 2010, 1991, 1986, 1970 Confraternity of Christian Doctrine, Washington, D.C., and are used by permission of the copyright owner. All rights reserved. No part of the *New American Bible* may be reproduced in any form without permission in writing from the copyright owner.

Excerpts from the English translation of the *Catechism of the Catholic Church* for use in the United States of America, copyright © 1994, United States Catholic Conference, Inc. — Libreria Editrice Vaticana. Used with permission.

Excerpts from papal and magisterium texts copyright © Libreria Editrice Vaticana. All rights reserved. Used with permission.

Cover design by Ryan McQuade

Published by Pauline Books & Media, 50 Saint Pauls Avenue, Boston, MA 02130-3491. www.pauline.org.

Printed in the U.S.A.

Pauline Books & Media is the publishing house of the Daughters of St. Paul, an international congregation of women religious serving the Church with the communications media.

1 2 3 4 5 6 7 8 9   24 23 22 21 20

For my wife, Grace.
You truly are amazing.

Contents

Foreword

THE HUMAN PERSON can survive only about three weeks without food. (Though working on a college campus makes me wonder if some of my students could survive more than three hours.)

Water is even more important for human survival. We can only live for a few days without water.

And then there's oxygen. Without oxygen we can only survive for a few minutes.

But, believe it or not, there's something even more essential to human life than food, water, or oxygen—hope. We can't live a moment without hope. Not one moment.

The human heart demands and longs for hope. We need hope to be fully alive and to live a life full of purpose, promise, peace, and joy. Sadly, however, many people live without this balm for the soul, which is so unfortunate because it doesn't have to be that way.

It doesn't help that many people confuse the virtue of hope with a desire or want. We often hear people say things like, "I hope the weather is nice on our vacation." Or, "I hope I get that job." While we use the word "hope" in these instances, we don't really hope for or in these things. We might want the weather to be nice on our vacation and we might even pray for that intention but is our hope really in a vacation? Or we might desire that job, but should we really *hope* in it?

Saint Paul tells us that "hope does not disappoint" (Rom 5:5). But how does that work? So often peoples' hopes are disappointed. However, when we experience disappointment, it's because we didn't have a clear understanding of hope. We didn't know where, or in whom, to place our hope. We need only look at today's world to see the consequences of many lives lived without real, authentic hope. Anxiety, frustration, addiction, confusion, angst —all this and more can come from a lack of real hope.

For this reason, Kris Frank's book on the topic of hope is so timely and important. In it, he does an excellent job illuminating our profound need for hope. He points out that true hope is found in Jesus Christ and in him alone. Hope anchored in God's love gives purpose and meaning to our lives. We all long for this kind of hope, the hope that brings light and reminds us that God is who he says he is; the hope that confirms that our present struggle is not the end. This is the only kind of true hope that will not disappoint. Today's world so profoundly needs to know the source of our hope. So, I encourage you to begin reading this book right away. There's not a minute to lose.

FATHER DAVE PIVONKA, TOR
President, Franciscan University

CHAPTER ONE

Hope

"Hold fast to the hope that lies before us. This we have as an anchor of the soul."

—Hebrews 6:18–19

ON JULY 4, 1952, Florence Chadwick set out to do something many deemed impossible. The 34-year-old planned to be the first woman to swim the Catalina Channel—a 21-mile stretch of water between Catalina Island and the California coast. That day the weather was abysmal. The water was bitterly cold, and a dense fog inhibited visibility. Nevertheless, Florence swam for hours. Support boats carrying her mother and trainer followed closely behind. Rifles were fired repeatedly to scare away sharks that stalked below. From warm and cozy homes around the country, many people watched with interest as the event played out on television. After swimming nearly sixteen hours, however, Florence was completely depleted and discouraged. She gave up and asked to be taken out of the water. Back in the boat, Florence realized she had been only 1/2 mile away from the shore. Afterward, Florence confessed to a reporter, "Look, I'm not excusing myself, but if I could have seen land, I know I could have made it."[1]

Most of us haven't swum the Catalina Channel (or any channel for that matter), but we all can relate to Florence's excuse for not getting to the finish line. Sometimes we go through life wondering, "How much longer can I strive for something I cannot see?" If only we could see the shoreline, it would be so much easier. Just staying afloat can seem impossible in the face of each day's never-ending, difficult moments. We fail and fall short; sometimes life becomes too difficult, and we want to call it quits. I often feel this way, and my guess is that I'm not alone. Actually, I *know* I'm not alone.

Over the years I've encountered countless people—young and old alike—who find it difficult to make it through life. Like Florence Chadwick, they feel like the shorelines of a happy, joyful life are perpetually just out of reach. We may not desire to swim long distances surrounded by sharks to earn some record, but God created each one of us for greatness. And like Florence, however, when life becomes arduous, we can easily become discouraged. Thankfully, even when we're surrounded by the dense fog of the unknown, there's a proven way to navigate the chilly, choppy waters of life. God provides us with something that anchors us when everything else threatens to blow us off course. In case it's not obvious, I'm talking about the virtue of hope.

In the supernatural sense, hope is not the positive emotion that might have helped Florence push through the last half mile to shore. Hope is not a feel-good optimism that helps people get through tough times. Rather, hope is a theological virtue, a gift from God given to us in Baptism. When properly understood and lived, the virtue of hope can save our lives. It can anchor us both when life is calm and effortless and also when it feels difficult and impossible. Living in Christian hope is not always easy, especially when the disruptions and distresses of life pile up, but it's possible. And it's worth it. In fact, it's exactly what helps us to not only survive but to thrive. Before we begin to explore how to live hope amid life's ups and downs, let's explore a bit more exactly what hope is and what it isn't.

Hope Defined

In everyday conversation, we often equate hope with a wish for the future. We say things like, "My birthday is coming up. I hope I get the new Apple watch" or "I hope the line at Chick-fil-A isn't too long." Growing up in Northwest Ohio, for example, I *hoped* that Cleveland's Browns would play well enough to eke out a few wins. (You may take this as a knock on Cleveland sports. Don't.

Those are my teams. I'll root for them through thick and thin. Rain or shine. Win or lose. . . . But to be honest, they mostly lose.) Now, let's be clear, it isn't necessarily wrong to hope in these ways. We all hope for a perfect birthday gift or that our favorite team pulls off a big upset—but when we hope for these things, we aren't exercising the virtue of hope.

The *Catechism of the Catholic Church* (*CCC*) tells us, "Hope is the theological virtue by which we desire the kingdom of heaven and eternal life as our happiness, placing our trust in Christ's promises and relying not on our own strength, but on the help of the grace of the Holy Spirit" (1817). I don't use the word "beautiful" to describe many definitions, but it seems appropriate here. Hope grants us the assurance that our deepest longings can and will be satiated by the God who put those desires within our hearts. The virtue gives us the supernatural strength to rely on Christ's grace when our own strength fails. Hope is what prompted Saint Catherine of Siena to proclaim, "All the way to heaven, is heaven."[2] Hope points our faith to eternal life and brings heaven, in some sense, into the present moment.

Hope is given to us in Baptism, but we are not mere passive recipients of this gift. Aided by grace, hope is a movement of the will. Of course, hope can provoke an emotional response, but fundamentally we have to choose to conform with the grace that has been given to us by God. Life is too difficult to passively stumble into hope. It's a virtue we must fight for with God's grace. When we live the virtue of hope, it leads us to happiness. Hope is the foundation of the joy that Christians are called to live in all circumstances. It's a life-changing gift that leads us to encounter God. When we live the virtue of hope in our lives, it completely changes the way we approach the world around us.

It's also important to realize that hope isn't a quick fix that immediately fulfills our longings and saves us from life's hardships. Instead, amid our aches and sufferings, hope keeps our gaze on Christ, confident in his promises. Too often we turn our focus away from the source of our hope—Jesus—and shift our gaze to earthly things. This shift may go unnoticed for a time. But when life takes a turn for the worse, a lack of hope can cripple us, which is why it's so important to actively ask God for the grace to grow in hope every day.

Hope in Everyday Life

A few years ago, I returned home from a long weekend away where I had been serving on a retreat for a local youth group. Being away from family is never easy, but this time was especially challenging. During the retreat, the camp's water pump broke, and the entire grounds were out of water for most of the weekend. We had no running water for cooking, showers, or toilets. We almost cancelled the event, but we decided to persevere. Thankfully, the retreat was a success. But after spending a long weekend running and playing in the humid Texas woods, I was ready to go home and take a nice, warm, long shower. My dreams of rest and relaxation, however, would soon be shattered. As I walked across my front lawn, I noticed my sneakers making a strange squishing sound. I looked down and realized that our grass was completely saturated in water from a broken pipe.

While waiting for the water department to arrive, I was consumed with frustration. I'm ashamed to say that my anger, combined with the fear of a hefty bill, led to a major freak-out. I ended up locking myself in the bathroom to escape the predicament for a minute and to collect myself. I had some choice words for God, and they weren't pretty. I was irate. I was incensed. Sure, it was just a broken pipe. I know that now and, to be honest, I knew it in the moment. The situation could have been so much worse. Even so, it all seemed so unfair. I couldn't understand why God would allow these water problems to follow me home.

Standing in my family's little bathroom, I couldn't reconcile how an all-loving, all-powerful, all-knowing God could let such an irksome and preventable thing happen. Now, was I facing a truly exasperating dilemma? Yes. A broken pipe needed to be fixed, and it was an inconvenience. My predicament was made even more inconvenient by my exhaustion and financial worries. In hindsight, however, the real issue wasn't a broken pipe. It was my broken perspective. My focus had fallen from the things of heaven to the stresses and annoyances of this world. And my shift in focus had left me completely unable to deal with what was a relatively small problem.

I'm sure most of you can relate to this ridiculous, rather embarrassing story. Most of us have been thrown

into a tizzy by pretty insignificant things. A friend doesn't
text us back quickly enough, and we lose our patience. A
family member says the wrong thing at the wrong time,
and we snap. A roommate pushes our buttons until we've
had enough. Someone on the interstate drives too fast, and
we give the person a one-finger salute. At times, the most
trivial events can provoke the ugliest behavior. Deep down,
however, most of us know that relatively minor problems
like these are not the worst things we'll have to face.
Inevitably the seasons of our lives will move from little
annoyances to far greater struggles. When we're reeling
from a family member's recent diagnosis, a broken pipe
seems less devastating. Or when we are heartbroken from
a recent breakup, we may barely notice a traffic jam that
would have left us irate on any other day.

Life's great sufferings put other sufferings in perspective. When we ask God for the grace to hope amid small
sufferings, it prepares us to hope when we face more sub-
stantial sorrows. If we aren't intentional and disciplined
about living hope, however, the small and large issues can
compound. Eventually, without hope, our little sufferings
can become a weight impossible to bear. This is why hope
is so vital. Whether facing daily inconveniences or significant suffering, if we lose our focus on God, our hearts can
begin to absorb and reflect the hardness and misery of our
trials rather than the love of Christ. Wherever we find
ourselves and whatever we are going through, the virtue of
hope helps us to trust that we will never be abandoned by
God in our time of need. Hope gives us the ability to raise
our gaze from our suffering to our Savior.

Jesus Is Our Hope

This chapter opened with a quote from the Letter to the Hebrews. Let's take a moment to read more of that passage:

> When God wanted to give the heirs of his promise an even clearer demonstration of the immutability of his purpose, he intervened with an oath, so that by two immutable things, in which it was impossible for God to lie, we who have taken refuge might be strongly encouraged to hold fast to the hope that lies before us. This we have as an anchor of the soul, sure and firm. (Heb 6:17–19)

In this passage, we learn that our hope is steadfast, grounded, and sure because it is rooted in the immutable promise and oath of our God. Without hope, the storms of life can cause us to drift away into an abyss of despair. Thankfully, God gave us hope that anchors us to him. With hope as our anchor, nothing can shake us. Our God is trustworthy. He will never leave, abandon, or forget us in times of need.

As Christians, hope is one of the most crucial gifts given by God to carry us through this life. Unfortunately, some of us believe the lie that hope cannot sustain us during life's most difficult events. If by hope we meant something like "good vibes," then this would be true. It would be silly to live in that kind of hope. We'd inevitably end up fools if we depended on something so vague. We all know that things turn out badly despite wishful thinking. Positive attitudes don't protect us from problems.

Hope isn't pie-in-the-sky optimism. Hope is much more grounded. It doesn't blindly assume the best even when things are horrible. Hope sees reality. Hope is neither nebulous nor ethereal. Emily Dickinson once wrote,

Hope is the thing with feathers
That perches in the soul
And sings the tune without the words
    And never stops at all.[3]

Though a beautiful sentiment, I disagree with the famed poet. This tune of hope does have words. In fact, our hope is *the* Word. Our hope is Jesus.

We have a God who was willing to become man. God the Father sent his Son to enter into our mire and muck. Jesus took on our humanity in all ways but sin. He knows what it is to feel lonely and angry. He understands our hurt, our brokenness, and our shame. He bore it all on a cross. He died a death he didn't deserve so that we could live eternal life with him, something we could never earn ourselves. Through the outpouring of the Holy Spirit in our Baptism, we are saved from our sins and given the gift of eternal life. At Baptism our souls are infused with the theological virtues of faith, hope, and love. These virtues center us on God and "[make us] capable of acting as [God's] children and of meriting eternal life" (*CCC* 1813). In other words, the theological virtues draw us into a deeper and richer relationship with God. Because of this wondrous mystery, we can place our hope in God. No matter what situation we face, hope assures us that our best days lie ahead.

Ways to Read This Book

My objective in writing this book is not to give a thorough theological breakdown of the virtue of hope. Many worthwhile resources do just that. Instead, I offer a field guide for the times in our lives when we most need hope by highlighting the specific hurdles that block our path to a hope-filled life. The first eight chapters focus on cultivating hope in our own lives while the final three examine how we can share hope with those around us. This book won't fix all our problems or give us all the answers our hearts are seeking. But, when read in combination with prayer, it will point us to a God who can.

Before reading any further, please allow me to offer a few suggestions for how to get the most out of this book.

A Simple Read

My idea of a perfect Saturday (or any day for that matter) is to be stretched out on a cozy couch with a cup of coffee and a good book. So if this book is just one on a long list of to-reads, then by all means, read it as you would read any other book. A book read is better than a book unread. But as you read, be sure to say a prayer asking God to help you to grow in the virtue of hope.

Group Study

Study groups and book clubs can really help us to absorb a book's content. People of different viewpoints, ideas, and lifestyles also can shine a brighter light on the

importance of hope for our world. So you might consider
inviting a friend to read along with you. Or, even better,
invite a group to gather and discuss the book. Each chapter ends with a few questions to help foster discussion and
reflection. These questions can serve as a springboard into
more in-depth conversations.

Personal Meditations

This book's chapters are not formatted as prayer med-
itations, but they still can be a companion to prayer. Try
taking this book with you to an adoration chapel or keep it
next to your favorite prayer spot at home. As you read each
chapter, give yourself the time and space to pray and
reflect. No need to rush. If any words, paragraphs, or ideas
strike a chord, take a break and pray for a bit. God has
something more for you than the words on these pages.
This book is a blueprint, but God is the actual architect
when it comes to your growth in hope.

However you choose to approach reading this book, I
pray that it's enjoyable and helps you to grow in the virtue
of hope.

CHAPTER TWO

Hope for the Sinner

"[God's] justice gives rise to fear but consideration of his mercy gives rise to hope." [1]

—SAINT THOMAS AQUINAS

I HAVE A confession to make.

Brace yourself.

Are you ready?

Here we go.

I'm a sinner. A big, fat sinner. I'm not proud of this reality, but it's true. This revelation has probably caused you some shock and mental distress, so feel free to take a few moments to recuperate. Now that my sinfulness is out in the open, I think it's only fair that you acknowledge your sinfulness too. Most of us don't like to admit our sin openly. But most of us can't deny it either. We all fall short of the glory of God. Don't worry, this isn't a shame session, just a reality check. In order to understand the hope in what Jesus has done for us, we first need to accept and examine the reality of our sin.

Now, you may be tempted to skim over this part of the book. We all know about sin. Almost everyone believes sin is bad. Some may debate what constitutes a sin, but most of us agree that sin in general should be avoided. The truth, however, is we can only appreciate the beauty of God's love and forgiveness to the degree that we comprehend the ugliness of our sin. So stick with me. By the end of this chapter, you will understand in a clearer way why, even in the midst of your sin, you still can have joyful hope.

No Sense in Sin

Years ago, I was invited to give some talks in Florida. As compensation for my time, I was offered a ticket to the Kennedy Space Center in Cape Canaveral. Now that might not be exciting to you, but I'm a *huge* space nerd. The universe fascinates me. (Seriously, if it doesn't impress you that we're standing on a rock orbiting the sun and traveling at a speed of 67,000 miles per hour, we probably can't be friends.) Needless to say, when I was offered a ticket to NASA's space launch complex, I couldn't pass up the incredible opportunity.

After a few days of ministry, it was finally time for my private excursion to the space center. I was almost giddy as

I arrived at the entrance line. When I finally made it to the front, I was courteously greeted by a kind, grandmotherly woman carefully scanning each ticket. Her polite smile faded as my ticket refused to scan. She tried it multiple times, but each attempt ended in failure. She was frustrated. I was vexed. I was also holding up the line, and the people behind me were becoming annoyed.

Stuck at the gate, as I looked longingly at other tourists entering the park, I barely noticed the ticket taker reexamine my ticket. Then her voice broke through my distracted thoughts, "Son, I'm so sorry, but I just realized your ticket is expired." Tears started to well up in my eyes. I wish I could blame it on the fact that I was tired from three days of ministry or that I was miles away from a family that I missed dearly, but ultimately, I just really wanted to see some space stuff. When the elderly woman saw my emotional state, her grandma skills kicked in. She hugged me, patted me on the back, and whispered, "Go on in. Just go. It will be our secret." That day I learned that you can never underestimate the power of a 28-year-old crying like a toddler in front of an 80-year-old. I also gained further insight into sin.

Sin is like an expired ticket. At first glance, it appears to promise happiness and seems like a shortcut toward fulfillment, but it only leads to a dead end. Sin impedes our entrance to eternal life and draws us further away from God. The Letter of James doesn't mince words when discussing sin: "Each person is tempted when he is lured and enticed by his own desire. Then desire conceives and brings forth sin, and when sin reaches maturity

it gives birth to death" (1:14–15). Sin never gives life; it
just takes it. Like a shiny, new lure, sin has a way of
appearing appetizing to us. If it weren't enticing, we
would never fall for the trap. And that's what makes
avoiding sin so tricky; it's a snare that humans have fallen
for since the beginning of time.

Of course, just because sin tempts us, doesn't mean we
have to take the bait. But it's also not always so easy to
resist. And it often doesn't help when someone responds
to our struggle by saying, "Just stop sinning!" Sure, we
should try to stop sinning, but we all know it's neither an
easy nor an instantaneous process. When we're caught up
in temptation, sin doesn't seem so bad. Sometimes sin is a
desire for bad things, but often sin makes us want good
things in the wrong way. Success, affirmation, recognition,
and sex are good things, but they make awful gods. When
they take the place of God, they become disruptive,
destructive, and, ultimately, dissatisfying. Sin promises
that something other than living for God will leave us satiated, but it never, ever does.

When we sin, we fail to place our hope in God.
Basically, sin is misplaced hope. Remember, the verse from
the Letter of James tells us that our "own desires" lead to
our downfall. That's not to say all our desires are bad, but
the misplaced ones can lead to sin. For example, we may
desire to avoid hurting another person's feelings, so we
make the choice to lie to get out of an awkward and difficult situation. Or, we may desire love and intimacy, so we
turn to pornography as a cheap and hollow substitute. Or,
we might desire to be successful and get ahead in life, so

we cheat or steal at school or work. It doesn't take much reflection to realize that all these scenarios never pan out the way we expect. Sin leaves us feeling hurt, damaged, and alone. And though sin affects us on a deeply personal level, we often aren't the only ones hurt by our decisions.

One time I was sitting with some teens after a retreat. We were discussing our weekend and most of the conversation was lighthearted. As we recalled some of the fun moments from the past few days, the group rocked with laughter. One of the girls, however, was somber and pensive. We had spoken during the retreat, and I knew she had recently made some poor decisions. I asked her what she was thinking, and I'll never forget her answer. Almost whispering, she responded, "I feel like I'm cheating on God. I've hurt God." While the rest of us were laughing, she was grappling with a truth that we must all come to grasp.

Sin is not just a matter of breaking impersonal rules— it's a matter of relationship. It's personal. Yes, sin is an offense against God's command. More importantly though, in breaking God's law we tragically break away from his love. Breaking relationship with God causes great pain and heartache. Once we have sinned, the Enemy wants us to believe there's no hope and that we're beyond redemption. But he's a liar. This break is never irreversible while we still have breath in our lungs.

Saint John Paul II once said, "We are not the sum of our weaknesses and failures; we are the sum of the Father's love for us and our real capacity to become the image of his Son." [2] Let that sink in for a moment. Do you believe it? Do you know that because God created you, you are fundamentally good? Do you know that your sin doesn't define you? Do you know that in God's eyes, you are not just a face in the crowd, you are not just tolerable, and you don't have to earn his love and recognition? You are truly and utterly lovable. You are God's child. No poor decision, no mistake, and no sin changes that. God extends his love to us even when we may not love him in return. He extends mercy even when we deserve punishment. Like the grandmotherly ticket lady at NASA, God gives us entrance into relationship with him even when we have an expired ticket. When we repent of our sin, God welcomes us back into relationship with him. We have hope because of Jesus Christ.

Know Mercy

Have you ever told yourself that you weren't going to sin anymore, but then found yourself right back in the same situation? It can be incredibly difficult to change our behavior. Sometimes it even seems impossible. To overcome sin in our lives, we first have to recognize the reality of our current sinful state. We are not strong enough to trounce sin on our own. No matter how determined or headstrong we might be, we aren't going to be able to set ourselves straight with our own strength and discipline. Sin is too alluring. Too tempting. So how do we change the broken desires of our hearts? It's not as difficult as one might think: we replace them with something more beautiful than sin. Remember the movie *Shrek*? Princess Fiona chose love and a lifetime of witty one-liners with Shrek over prestige and looks. Similarly, in Shakespeare's *Romeo and Juliet*, as soon as Romeo lays eyes on Juliet, he forgets all about his crush, Rosaline. To truly overcome sin, God can replace our disordered desires with a desire for something greater, something better, something that will truly satisfy. Or rather, Someone.

We can look to the saints as an example. Before he met Christ, Saint Matthew was a dishonest tax collector, a traitor to his own people. Saint Paul terrorized and murdered Christians before he encountered Jesus on the road to Damascus. Saint Mary Magdalene was possessed by demons. Saint Francis of Assisi was a rich, spoiled kid who was no stranger to the party scene. Saint Augustine had a mistress and did not want to give up premarital sex. The list goes on and on. Many of the saints' lives were steeped in sin before they became the holy men and women we now know them to be. Though each of their stories is distinct, one thing they all had in common was that they didn't just turn away from their sin—they turned to Christ. Of course, once they turned to God it's not as if they never sinned again. But the saints' desire for Christ overwhelmed their desire for sin. And that changes everything.

We know that sin is bad news. Thankfully, the Gospel of Jesus Christ brings Good News: sin has been defeated. Christ has overcome sin and death and has paved a path for us to holiness and salvation. No crime is too great, no offense too severe for God's mercy. In Jesus, there is hope for even the most egregious sinner. This isn't spiritual fluff or holy hyperbole. It's Gospel truth. We see the reality of

Jesus' mercy in action in the last chapter of the Gospel of John. Before we get into the text, let's set up the scene. At this point, Jesus has been arrested, crucified, and died. His closest friends deserted him in his hour of need. Further, Peter, the head of the Apostles, denied Jesus three times, lying to and cursing those who accused him of being Jesus' friend. Peter messed up, and he knew it.

Fortunately for us, John recorded the moment when Peter and the resurrected Jesus were reunited. In John 21, Peter gathers up his boys for a little night fishing, only to catch nothing. (I'm really glad the whole "pope-thing" worked out for Peter because it seems he was not the most skilled of fishermen.) Just as the disciples are about to call it a night, a man calls out from shore to ask if they caught any fish. The disciples don't recognize the man at first, but it's Jesus. After hearing that they had caught nothing, Jesus commands them to cast their nets to the right of the boat. The disciples humor him and do as he says. Almost immediately, they bring in a monster haul of fish. Does this sound familiar? Almost the exact same thing happened in the Gospel of Luke at the beginning of Jesus' ministry (see 5:1–11). Jesus is repeating the miracle he worked when he first called Peter to follow him.

As the Apostles struggle to pull the fish into the boat, they recognize that the man on the shore is Jesus. Peter, overwhelmed with enthusiasm, dives off the boat and starts swimming to Jesus. When Peter reaches the beach, God's mercy and love are on full display for us. The haul of fish must have reminded Peter of Jesus' first invitation to follow him. Now Jesus' actions recall another memory, one that Peter probably wants to forget. Jesus is cooking breakfast on a charcoal fire. Only twice in the entire Bible do we see a charcoal fire: here on the beach and a few chapters prior when Peter denied Christ. Peter undoubtedly understands what is happening. He is standing by another charcoal fire, this time next to the man whom he had denied days earlier. Jesus' response is anything but expected:

> When they had finished breakfast, Jesus said to Simon Peter, "Simon, son of John, do you love me more than these?" He said to him, "Yes, Lord; you know that I love you." He said to him, "Feed my lambs." He then said to him a second time, "Simon, son of John, do you love me?" He said to him, "Yes, Lord, you know that I love you." He said to him, "Tend my sheep." He said to him the third time, "Simon, son of John, do you love me?" Peter was distressed that he had said to him a third time, "Do you love me?" and he said to him, "Lord, you know everything; you know that I love you." [Jesus] said to him, "Feed my sheep." . . . And when he had said this, he said to him, "Follow me." (Jn 21:15–17, 19)

Jesus recalls Peter's three denials by inviting Peter three times to reaffirm his love and hope in him.

Peter now has a choice: reject Christ's mercy and forgiveness or recommit to following Christ and know his mercy intimately. Peter could have allowed his sin to define him. Luckily for us, Peter chose to be defined by his hope in God's love and mercy.

Sacrament of Hope

Like Peter, we too can choose hope. Forgiveness and mercy are always available to us. Always. As Catholics, we can experience God's mercy in an incredibly palpable and tangible way in the sacraments of Baptism and Reconciliation. According to the *Catechism of the Catholic Church*, "Through Baptism we are freed from sin and reborn as sons of God; we become members of Christ, are incorporated into the Church and made sharers in her mission" (1213). Of course, after Baptism our inclination to sin remains. So we must turn to the sacrament of Reconciliation when we have sinned to renew and strengthen our baptismal grace.

Some have a hard time accepting the importance of confession, but this sacrament is a gift from Jesus. After his resurrection, Jesus breathed on the Apostles and said to them, "Receive the holy Spirit. Whose sins you forgive are forgiven them, and whose sins you retain are retained" (Jn 20:22–23). In this scene, Jesus is giving the Apostles the authority to forgive sins in his place. This authority has been handed on from the Apostles to other priests through ordination. Therefore, the priest who hears our confessions extends Christ's own forgiveness. Priests are given the grace when they are ordained to act in the person of Christ, or *in persona Christi*, when administering the sacraments. Of course, special configuration to Christ does not make a priest perfect or sinless. It simply guarantees that when he administers the sacraments we will receive God's grace. Therefore, when we confess our sins to a priest and he gives us absolution, we can be confident that we will receive God's mercy and forgiveness. The sacrament of Reconciliation is a concrete way to experience God's mercy.

Saint Augustine once wrote, "So long as he bears the flesh, man cannot but have some light sins. But do not make light of these sins that we call light. If you make light of them when you weigh them, be afraid when you count them. Many light sins make one huge sin: many drops fill the river; many grains make the lump. And what hope is there? Before all, confession."[3] As Augustine points out, the sacrament of Reconciliation not only extends mercy to us, it also extends hope. When we receive the theological virtues through Baptism, we can lose or render them lifeless through serious sin. Reconciliation resuscitates the virtue of hope. Through it, we not only receive God's forgiveness but consolation, peace, and grace to fight future temptations. The battle to live in hope is never easy, but God's grace will assist us. Through this sacrament of forgiveness, we can repent of our sin, restore our broken relationship with God, and recapture lost hope.

Whatever temptations we're facing or sins we're committing, we know that God's mercy and grace are not far from us. As Saint Paul once wrote in his Letter to the Romans, "Where sin increased, grace overflowed all the more" (5:20). The sacrament of Reconciliation has the power to break every chain of sin that prevents us from being who we were designed to be. We worship a God of forgiveness and mercy. A God of fresh starts. A God of second chances, third chances, and even a million chances if we're willing to come before God with a contrite and humble heart. Pope Francis reminds us, "God never tires of forgiving us; we are the ones who tire of seeking his mercy."[4] We shouldn't let sin rob us of our hope. With Jesus, there's always hope for the sinner. For sinners like you and me, that's Good News.

Discussion Questions

1. What do you think makes sin so alluring? Do certain sins tempt you more than others? Why do you think that's the case?

2. What are some practical ways the gift of the virtue of hope can help you to combat sin?

3. What are some concrete ways you could try to lean into God's mercy this week?

CHAPTER THREE

Hope for the Discouraged

"Do not give in to discouragement, do not resign yourself to ways of thinking and living that have no future because they are not based on the solid certainty of God's Word!"[1]

—Saint John Paul II

LAST CHRISTMAS, MY oldest daughters, Magdalene and Eden, were given a special gift from Santa. They each received a set of building blocks—think Legos but smaller, pink, and easier to lose. My kids were thrilled. I was less so. These toys don't assemble themselves, and I had a hunch who the girls were going to ask for help. Now, I love playing with my kids, and I enjoyed playing with Legos when I was their age. But these monstrosities were much more complicated and—not to sound dramatic or anything—they contained about a zillion pieces that needed constructing.

Fast forward three hours later, and I'm coming undone. As I struggled to properly assemble the toys, the only thing building was my frustration. I thought I was never going to finish. The instructions weren't helping. Pieces were missing. Color schemes were somehow messed up. Sections I had already pieced together were falling and breaking apart. To add to the pressure, my eager daughters were watching closely and obsessively asking me why my structure didn't look like the picture on the front of the box. Putting together a child's toy should not have been that discouraging, but it was. I didn't realize it then, but that Christmas night, surrounded by toys made for pre-schoolers, God was moving in my heart.

Later, as I reflected on how disheartened I had become, I realized that the discouragement I had been feeling was familiar. I often feel like I am trying (and failing) to piece together various elements of my life: school, career, friends, family, Church. The list goes on and on. Despite my best efforts, the pieces of my life don't fit together in the way I want. My reality doesn't match my aspirations (with the obvious exception of my drop-dead gorgeous wife and beautiful children, of course).

Caleb's Hope

One of the reasons I love the Bible is that it's chock-full of characters who experienced the same ups and downs

of life that we face today. Lots of people have favorite
Bible characters, such as Abraham, David, or maybe Peter
or the Apostles. My favorite is Caleb. Compared to other
biblical figures, Caleb isn't a central player by any stretch
of the imagination. He refused, however, to allow discouragement to detract from his hope. (He's also a spy, which
is pretty cool).

Caleb's story begins in the Book of Numbers. He was
among the Israelites who followed Moses into the desert
after years of captivity in Egypt. Searching for a new home
to call their own, the Israelites came upon the land of
Canaan. God then told Moses to send men to explore the
Promised Land that he was giving to them. Caleb was
selected as a spy, along with eleven other men, to scout out
their future home. For forty days they infiltrated and
explored the land and saw that it was all they had wished
for and more—abundantly fruitful and beautiful. The men
later described the land to Moses saying, "It does indeed
flow with milk and honey" (Nu 13:27). Ten of the spies,
however, told Moses that victory in battle was hopeless, as
the cities were well-fortified and the inhabitants were
giants. In the spies' discouragement, they exaggerated
their reports to Moses and the Israelites; they were afraid
of what would happen if they tried to enter the land as
God had commanded.

But Caleb and another spy, Joshua, spoke in truth
against the other men's cowardice. Just as God's chosen
people were making plans to return to Egypt, Caleb spoke:

> The land which we went through and reconnoitered is
> an exceedingly good land. If the LORD is pleased with

us, he will bring us in to this land and give it to us, a
land which flows with milk and honey. Only do not
rebel against the LORD! You need not be afraid of the
people of the land, for they are but food for us! Their
protection has left them, but the LORD is with us. Do
not fear them. (Num 14:7–9)

Can you picture it? It's like a scene from a movie.
Everyone is ready to pack up and leave just as they are at
the front door of the Promised Land. They figure giving
up is way easier than facing inevitable trouble and hardship. But Caleb won't accept retreat. He knows the risks.
He knows the land is filled with powerful armies and fortified cities. Nonetheless, Caleb, the classic underdog,
stands to rouse the people to stand and fight. He reminds
the Israelites that the land is good, but more importantly,
he reminds them that God is good.

Caleb knew the people would face adversity, but he
also knew God would not abandon them. With God on
their side, he had confidence that the Israelites could
devour any poor chump who would dare stand in their
way. I like to think that if I had heard Caleb's courageous
speech I would have rallied to fight. Sadly, the Israelites
did not. Instead, they tried to kill Caleb. Fortunately,
though the Israelites weren't impressed by him, God was.
Because of the Israelites' lack of trust, God decided that
they would be banished to wander the desert for forty
years. The people would be unable to return to Canaan
until an entire generation had died out; only then would
God bring his people back to the Promised Land. The

Lord decided that Caleb and Joshua, however, would survive their time in the desert due to their faithfulness.

Now, we don't know what it's like to face fortified Canaanite cities. And, hopefully, we haven't wandered in a desert for forty years. But we've all felt discouraged in the face of insurmountable odds. So how should we respond in the face of seemingly hopeless situations? You know what I'm talking about, right? Maybe you feel like you will never earn a good grade in school. You wonder whether you'll ever get a promotion. You are single and losing confidence that you'll find "the one." Maybe you're ill, and the doctors don't know the cause or cure. Or, you can't piece together building blocks designed for children. Discouragement can vary in severity, but we all have moments when we didn't get what we want or expect.

Without even realizing it, discouragement can creep into our lives like a rain cloud and block any ray of light that hope offers. After all, life is hard sometimes. We all experience feeling lonely and misunderstood. We all have times when we wonder whether things will ever turn around, or whether it's even worth trying. When things don't go our way, discouragement takes hold of our hearts, and we naturally want to quit. We give up trying to focus on God and achieve the greatness for which our hearts long. And soon we settle for inferior things, which seem less daunting and more attainable but are also less satisfying. When we give into discouragement, we let go of dreams that seem out of reach, and we settle for the mundane and mediocre.

Surprisingly, worldly distractions aren't always what trip us up. Sometimes our spiritual efforts can leave us dispirited. Jesus commanded us in the Gospel of Matthew, "Be perfect, just as your heavenly Father is perfect" (5:48). Perfect? That's a tall order. I can't speak for you, but, if anything, I'm the perfect image of *imperfection*. I try to be kind and morally upright, but I'm horribly flawed. Do you feel this way too? For example, have you ever been dismayed to find an old sin you thought was long gone that has found its way back into your life? Maybe your prayer life that used to be fruitful is now dry and tedious. Maybe you feel like your regular church groups and Bible studies are getting boring and unremarkable or that great resolution you made to frequent the sacraments has dissipated. Mass has become a chore, and you can't remember the last time you went to confession.

When life disappoints, we can begin to think that God is disappointing. We look up to the heavens and scream, "Not fair!" But God is not about dispensing easy fixes and favors as if he were a cosmic vending machine. And Catholicism is not a list of spiritual dos and don'ts that, if followed correctly, magically grant us earthly bliss. We could cry out to God and expect repayment for all our good works as if God were all about karma. But Almighty God is not to be approached with a quid pro quo mentality. When we take this approach, we set ourselves up for a lifetime of discontent. God never promised a comfortable life for his followers, but what he offers is so much better. Therefore, to overcome discouragement, we need to recapture and realign our hope. Awards, accolades, ribbons, and trophies cannot be the objects of our hope. If we place hope in the things of this world, we'll be let down. And if we set our hopes on our spiritual merits and works, we'll still find ourselves disappointed. Only when we place our hope in God can we be sustained through any situation.

God Has Plans for You

A Scripture passage that gives more peace than a cell phone with a fully charged battery is Jeremiah 29:11. Here, God speaks through the prophet saying, "For I know well the plans I have in mind for you . . . plans for your welfare and not for woe, so as to give you a future of hope." Perhaps you've come across this passage before. It's a good one. If you hang around church groups long enough, I bet you'll be given a t-shirt or coffee mug with this verse printed on it. And rightfully so. It's an outstanding promise from God; his words are uplifting and assuring. God has a plan for us. We are not here by accident. God knows us better than we know ourselves and is looking out for us. Jeremiah assures us that God has a purpose for our lives, even when we can't see it.

Once, I was speaking at a conference, and two youth ministers asked me to talk to a teen named Theresa. They told me that she was sick and could use some support and encouragement. Little did I know that it would be Theresa who would be offering encouragement and hope to me. When I first saw her, Theresa was tired and pale, confined to a wheelchair, and wrapped in a blanket. But she greeted me with a smile and warmth that didn't match her physical state. As we chatted, she told me that she felt perpetually dizzy. Because of this, walking was nearly impossible and eating made her nauseous. Through the entire conversation, she never once complained or showed an ounce of annoyance about her situation. I invited Theresa to meet and pray with the speaking team that evening.

That night, as the team gathered for prayer, we waited for Theresa to arrive. And, let me tell you, she definitely made an entrance. Her entourage of about fifteen family members and friends would have made Kanye West jealous. We all crammed in the room with Theresa at the center. Her enthusiasm and vigor for life were palpable. As we chatted, she filled in a few more gaps regarding her health condition. She was undiagnosed. One day she had laid down to take a nap, and when she woke up, her world was spinning—literally. Just like that, her life was changed forever. She shared her story with tears in her eyes. Her pain and frustration were a constant companion; her longing for relief ever present. At the same time, Theresa's hope in Jesus graced her every word. Her wheelchair had become a podium, and though she did not give a formal talk, her message was heard loud and clear: there's no room for lasting discouragement when you are following an everlasting God.

As we moved into a time of prayer, we gathered around Theresa's wheelchair, laid hands on her, and asked the Holy Spirit to heal her mysterious ailment. We pleaded with God for her pain to subside and that she would regain the ability to walk. As we prayed, I was convinced God was going to heal Theresa on the spot. I even prayed with my eyes open because I wanted to see the moment the miracle occurred. I wish I could report that God physically healed Theresa that day. I wish I could say that I saw her stand up and start dancing right there in the middle of our prayer circle. But she didn't. If anyone ever had a reason to be discouraged in that moment, it was Theresa. No one would have blamed her if she were. But she wasn't. Her hope was not in a miraculous healing but in God.

Hope tells us that even when our problems outnumber us 100 to 1, God is on our side. Saint Paul assures us, "We know that all things work for good for those who love God, who are called according to his purpose" (Rom 8:28). Maybe you are in a senseless situation. Perhaps you are dealing with a hardship or vice that you fear will be your undoing. Whatever you are experiencing, remember that God is a master of turning messes into masterpieces. He can take your garbage and gunk and use it for the Gospel. Just because your plans haven't panned out the way you thought, doesn't mean that God's plans have been derailed. Maybe you wish God would pamper you. But what if he is preparing you? Trust that God has you right where he needs you. No matter what happens, God can use it for your good. As the prophet Jeremiah said, God has plans for your life, and your future is one of hope.

Hope amid Discouragement

Hope isn't a one-time choice. It's a virtue that must be cultivated with God's grace each day. Living hope doesn't mean we'll never feel overwhelmed again. There's no way around discouraging situations. Jesus told us we would face them, "In the world you will have trouble" (Jn 16:33). But Jesus also tells us in that same verse, "Take courage, I have conquered the world." As hope redirects our gaze to Christ, it changes the way we experience the difficult present. We can find hope amid difficulty. Let's take a quick look at a few ways we can discover and grow in hope to safeguard against discouragement.

First and foremost, in seasons of dejection, we can turn to prayer. We turn to our Father to ask for what we need, but also to give thanks for what God has already given us. The Book of Ecclesiastes reminds us, "'What the eyes see is better than what the desires wander after.' This also is vanity and a chase after wind" (6:9). (Translation: It's better to be happy with what we have than miserable about what we don't.) We may not like where we currently are, but we probably aren't where we used to be either. Myriads of people used to visit Blessed Solanus Casey, a gentle, gaunt Capuchin priest, seeking intercession for their illnesses and problems. He would assure the people of his prayers and instruct them, "Thank God ahead of time!"[2] Thanking God before he answers (or doesn't answer) our prayers helps us to grow in hope and in trust as we acknowledge that his plans are better than ours.

In addition to prayer, in times of discouragement, we can turn to the Bible for consolation. Sacred Scripture is the word of God inspired by the Holy Spirit. Though written thousands of years ago, the word of God is still applicable in today's world. Saint Paul writes, "For whatever was written previously was written for our instruction, that by endurance and by the encouragement of the scriptures we might have hope" (Rom 15:4). That is to say, in times when hope feels lost, we can lean into Scripture. I'm not the best at being silent, so it can be a struggle to hear God speaking in prayer. When I long to hear God speak, I prayerfully open the word of God. In the midst of struggle, Scripture is a tangible reminder that God is good, always present, faithful, and approachable.

Speaking of Scripture, let's go back to the story of Caleb. After the Israelites wander the desert for nearly half a century, we get another glimpse of our hero. Forty years after wandering in the desert, Caleb returns to the Promised Land. The bad guys are still there. Peril and tribulation still lie ahead. And, just as before, Caleb is composed and collected. He attests to the faithfulness of God saying,

> I was forty years old when Moses, the servant of the Lord, sent me from Kadesh-barnea to reconnoiter the land; and I brought back to him a frank report. My fellow scouts who went up with me made the people's confidence melt away, but I was completely loyal to the Lord, my God. . . . Now, as he promised, the Lord has preserved me these forty-five years since the Lord spoke thus to Moses while Israel journeyed in the wilderness; and now I am eighty-five years old, but I am still as strong today as I was the day Moses sent me forth, with no less vigor whether it be for war or for any other tasks. Now give me this mountain region which the Lord promised me that day, as you yourself heard.

True, the Anakim are there, with large fortified cities,
but if the LORD is with me I shall be able to dispossess
them, as the LORD promised." (Jos 14:7–8; 10–12)

Despite years of wandering in the desert, Caleb's hope
remains unwavering because his hope is anchored in God's
unwavering promise.

Both Caleb and Theresa are models who remained
anchored in hope even when they could have easily given
into discouragement. They knew that they could trust
God completely even though their circumstances sug-
gested otherwise. God is powerful. And if he does not
change our difficult circumstances, we can trust that he
will use them for our good. Whatever kinds of discouragement we might face today, if we place our trust in God,
hope will triumph.

Discussion Questions

1. Can you think of a time in your life when discouragement seemed unyielding? How did you respond?
   How could you have responded better with the help
   of God's grace?

2. Why do you think God allows bad things to happen
   to us? How is hope related to our suffering?

3. What are some things that help you to maintain
   hope when life's circumstances make it extremely
   difficult?

CHAPTER FOUR

Hope for the Doubters

"To believe with certainty, one has to begin by doubting."[1]
—SHELDON VANAUKEN

I'VE BEEN BEWILDERED and dumbfounded many times while serving the Church. Once, despite repeated assurances, a woman refused to believe I was Catholic because I had referenced the Bible several times in a talk. Another time, in an attempt to win a retreat talent show, a teen thought it would be a good idea to pee his pants on stage in front of everyone. (We all lost that night.) But something that truly perplexes me is how impressionable people seem. I've even noticed this in my own experience teaching. I wish I could chalk it up to that fact that I'm a hip, silver-tongued, gifted orator, but I'm pretty sure it's

not that. Instead, what I've come to realize is that sometimes we can fall into a false comfort. Either we aren't
thinking seriously about the material being taught, or we
fear looking foolish for our doubts and struggles.

Once during a Bible study, a young adult asked me
whether Jesus should be considered Jewish or Christian. A
great question. But I can be a jerk sometimes, so I decided
to throw him a curveball. Instead of giving a sincere
answer, I jokingly replied that Jesus was actually an atheist.
The young man was clearly surprised by my response. But
I was equally surprised when I realized that the group was
just nodding mindlessly in agreement. After a few awkward moments, I said that I was just kidding. In everyone's
defense, it was an awful joke. My jokes are usually funnier.
(Ok, not really.) But that night left an impression on me.
What if I had never corrected myself and given them a
truthful answer? Could some of them really have left the
room thinking that Jesus, the Son of God, was actually an
atheist?

Doubt is often characterized as something negative in
relation to faith. But when I was teasing the young adults
at the Bible study, a doubtful response on their part would
have been healthy. Of course, doubt isn't always a good
response. If we give doubt precedence over faith, it can
lead to hopelessness and disbelief. We can, however, have
faith and at the same time have questions. In fact, if we are
thoughtful about our faith we *will* have questions. We'll
wonder about things like, "How does God exist if nothing
created him? Why does God allow bad things to happen
to good people? Why doesn't God work more miracles?"

At other times, doubt can produce far more personal questions like, "Is God listening to my prayers? Has God really forgiven my sins? Does God care about me? Does God really love me unconditionally or does he just tolerate me?" And sometimes we might even wonder, "Could this whole faith thing be a lie?" These questions are important, but how we go about answering them will determine whether our hope will grow or wither.

Doubt and Hope

For some of us who grew up in and around the Church, we learned that faith gives us certainty about what is true. That's not wrong, however many of us also may have picked up the incorrect idea that doubt is therefore unacceptable. If never corrected, this assumption can be detrimental to our spiritual growth and our capacity for hope. The reality is that doubt doesn't always have a negative impact on faith. To help us understand the nature of doubt, let's examine how the Church, in her wisdom, defines it.

The *Catechism of the Catholic Church* classifies two categories of doubt: voluntary and involuntary. Voluntary doubt sounds something like this: "I know what God says about what's right and wrong, and I understand Church teaching and why it's there. But I don't agree with or like the Church teaching, so it isn't for me." This line of thinking is less actual questioning and more an assertion of what we are and are not willing to accept as true. I'm not addressing this type of doubt in this chapter. Involuntary doubt creates questions more along the lines of, "How can this be? I don't get it. I don't understand. What does this mean for me and others?" Believe it or not, these kinds of questions have great potential to contribute to our faith lives. When we experience involuntary doubt, it's a sign that we're engaging and wrestling with our faith. In reference to this kind of doubt, Pope Francis once said, "Doubts that touch the faith, in a positive way, are a sign that we want to know better and more fully God, Jesus, and the mystery of his love for us."[2]

When we have questions about our faith, we can be certain that God can use our questions to enliven our hope rather than harm it. Our uncertainties, confusion, or spiritual hesitancies, rather than leading us into faith paralysis, can drive us to truth analysis. As the Letter to the Hebrews reminds us, "faith is the assurance of things hoped for, the conviction of things not seen" (11:1 NRSV). So, we can approach our doubts with faith, knowing that we will arrive at the truth.

Reasonable Faith

Created in God's image, we have been given an intellect and the ability to reason. What better way to use it than to ponder our faith? Saint Augustine once wrote, "I believe, in order to understand; and I understand, the better to believe."[3] Of course, some argue that faith is altogether unreasonable. They see it as a mere crutch that simpleminded people use to explain away what they can't understand. As Mark Twain wrote, "Faith is believing what you know ain't so."[4] Some Christians go to the opposite extreme and reject reason altogether, arguing that faith does not need to be reasonable.

Neither of these viewpoints properly describe the Catholic approach to faith and reason. The Catholic faith accepts that God's revelation of himself extends beyond human reason, but it does not nullify it. Faith and reason are not contradictory, they actually go together like peanut butter and jelly (or like bacon and just about anything else). Reason, therefore, is actually the common ground between believers and nonbelievers. Yet, some still argue against the credibility of the Christian faith and continue to claim that faith is unreasonable. For instance, atheists often argue that belief in God is irrational. In contrast, the Church teaches that by using one's reason, it is possible to reach belief in God. For centuries, great thinkers have provided us with reasonable proofs for the existence of God. Certainly, not everyone has the skills and training to philosophically reason their way to God's existence in a precise way. Nonetheless, many people can reason that just as a painting necessitates an artist or a wooden chair requires a carpenter, creation demands a Creator.

To believe with certainty that the world necessitates a Creator is reasonable. Basic logic tells us that nothing cannot generate something. And if we examine our surroundings a bit more carefully, we can gather even more characteristics of God. The complexity of life shows us that God is a God of order and not randomness. The universal and basic understanding of right and wrong, written on our hearts since creation, reveals that God is the source of goodness and morality. In the end, no matter how a person comes to believe in God, our faith—the basis of our hope—helps us to accept all the truths revealed by God.

This can seem complicated, but it doesn't have to be. Imagine for a moment that you are scrolling through Facebook and you come across a friend's photo. Next to your friend, you spot a girl who looks interesting. You decide to do some detective work. You click on her profile and start looking at her posts. Next, you look at her photos. Eventually, you find all her other social media accounts. An hour later, you realize that you've just spent a lot of time exploring a stranger's life. You've learned a lot, but you still can't claim that you *know* this girl. You'd be foolish to believe that everything one can know about a person can be known through an online profile. You may know her birthday, but you don't know how she prefers to spend it. You may see that she enjoys the outdoors, but you might not know why or how that interest began. At some point, if you are truly interested in knowing someone, you have to meet the person and spend real time together.

The same is true in our relationship with God. We can only garner so much information about God through reason. At a certain point we need something more. We need relationship. That's why, throughout history, God gradually revealed more of himself and his plan of salvation. Recorded in the Old and New Testaments, God's revelation through word and deed culminated and ended with the Incarnation of Jesus Christ. Jesus taught the Apostles all that he wished to reveal to us. This revelation has been preserved and interpreted by the Church, specifically by the bishops, the successors of the Apostles. Faith gives us access to truth about God that our natural reason would not have come to on its own. These truths do not negate what we can know through natural reason about God, but they build upon them. For example, reason can bring one to believe God exists, but only faith can bring one to believe that God is three Persons. Or we can know God is the Creator of the world through reason, but only faith reveals that he created the world from nothing and out of love.

Divine revelation from God gives our faith a certainty that natural reason does not have. When we accept divine revelation, our faith elevates our reason and takes us further into the complexity of truth than our human mind could have done on its own. Therefore, divine revelation, while it doesn't contradict reason, is superior to it. When we have difficulty understanding the truths of our faith, this doesn't mean they're untrue. It just means we're human. Faith goes beyond the reaches of our human intellect, but it also enriches it. When we use both faith and reason in harmony with one another, we will seek and find the one who is Truth itself: Jesus Christ.

Living Hopeful Faith

Sometimes I think that this whole faith thing would be a lot easier at times if only I could see Jesus heal a leper or walk on water. When I look at Scripture, however, I am comforted when I realize that those with front-row seats to Jesus' miracles and teachings still struggled with doubts. In the Gospel of John, for example, Jesus raises someone from the dead and people still did not believe in him. Take a moment to imagine this scene. Jesus receives word that his friend Lazarus is dying. By the time Jesus and the Apostles arrive, Lazarus is long gone—dead for four days to be exact. Finally, Jesus arrives and works a mighty miracle. He prays to the Father and calls out to Lazarus. Immediately, the dead man comes sauntering out of his tomb, wrapped in burial garb like a mummy from an old horror movie.

A man was dead. And then he wasn't. Things like that don't happen often. If I had witnessed Jesus raise someone from the dead, I'd like to think that my doubts would be gone for good. And yet, the next verse reveals that this miraculous marvel wasn't enough for some: "Now many of the Jews who had come to Mary and seen what [Jesus] had done began to believe in him" (Jn 11:25). When I first read this verse, I couldn't get past one, seemingly insignificant, word—"many." Many? Shouldn't the word be "all"? Why wouldn't *everyone* have come to believe in Jesus after such a marvelous feat? Yet, for some present that day, somehow doubt remained.

If people questioned Jesus after seeing him raise a dead man from the grave, one might wonder, "What chance do I have to believe without having seen Jesus work miracles?" We can find solace in the fact that many biblical figures struggled to comprehend the presence of the Son of God in their midst. Even the most significant players in Jesus' life were confused and had questions. Mary the mother of Jesus—born without sin—questioned how she could carry Christ in her womb while she was still a virgin (see Lk 1:34). Throughout the Gospels, in fact, Mary often pondered the workings of God in her life. Even John the Baptist, the one whom Jesus claimed was greater than any man ever born of woman (see Mt 11:11), was confused by Jesus. When John was in prison, he even doubted whether Jesus was the Messiah (see Mt 11:2–3). The Apostle Thomas, perhaps the most famous doubter of all time, is another hopeful example for us. Though most known for his doubt in the resurrected Lord, we often forget that Thomas was the first Apostle to make the clear declaration of faith in Jesus as God when he said, "My Lord and my God" (Jn 20:28).

The holy people in the Gospels who experienced confusion and doubt remind us that faith is a gift from God. Paul says as much in his First Letter to the Corinthians. When speaking of the seed of faith, he writes, "I planted, Apollos watered, but God caused the growth" (1 Cor 3:6). We don't earn faith. We can't will it or conjure it from thin air. Instead, we must receive it. The virtue of faith is given to every baptized person, but it's also up to us how we will use and develop it. When we trustingly ask God to increase our faith, this strengthens our hope and safeguards us from destructive doubts.

All this talk about faith and doubt may seem a bit abstract, but it's actually quite practical. I'll share one last example with you that illustrates the relationship between faith and doubt. I once sat on an airplane next to a woman who was close to hyperventilating the entire flight. Every bump, noise, or ring of a call bell made her jump. She obviously was horrified of flying. Every time something startled her, she'd clamp her eyes shut, swallow a muffled shriek, and squeeze my hand. She had a grasp that could crack a walnut. I tried to assure, reassure, encourage, and even distract her from her fear, but it didn't work. She doubted that she would get through the experience of flying, and I could do nothing to help her. I was nervous the first time I flew too. When we don't know how planes work or whether we can trust the mechanics, flying can be frightening. But as I flew more and more, my fears and doubts began to dissipate, and my trust in the engineers, pilots, and airlines grew.

The same can be true in our everyday lives. When we first experience doubts, it can be terrifying, just as it was for the woman who was afraid of flying. Doubts are often confusing and frightening. They reveal to us that we don't have all the answers and that we aren't in control. But as long as we trust that our loving God *is* in control, we will be able to survive the uncertain flight of life. Just like passengers on a plane, all Christians are on a journey. Some of us are at different points, but we're all trying to get to the same destination. Doubts will cause internal turbulence along the way, but we will make it if we allow God to serve as our pilot. Fear and doubt won't ever magically disappear, but living in faith and hope does lead us to more peace. Fueled by faith, we can trust that our hope will take flight and bring us to the destination of eternal life.

Saint Paul encouraged the early Church, "Test everything; retain what is good" (1 Thes 5:21); that is an imperative sentence. So we not only have permission to ask questions, we're obligated to ask them. If you have questions and uncertainties concerning the faith, search for answers! Look in the *Catechism*, read the Bible, ask a fellow Catholic you trust, or search for a faithful Catholic website. People have lived the Catholic faith for over two thousand years. Chances are good that at some point someone has asked the same questions you're asking. If you're willing to look, you'll find an answer.

Discussion Questions

1. What is an area in your faith life where you experience doubts?

2. Can you think of a time when God has used your doubts to strengthen your faith?

3. When someone you know struggles with doubt, how do you try to share hope with them?

CHAPTER FIVE

Hope for the Anxious

"Nothing in the affairs of men is worthy of great anxiety" [1]

—Plato

SEVERAL YEARS AGO, my family traded in our flip-flops for cowboy boots as we moved from Florida to Texas. I love Texas. But I think it's fair to say that the state did not like me. Don't get me wrong, I was beyond excited to move to the South to live out my cowboy fantasies and stuff myself with all the glorious Tex-Mex I could eat. And, for the first six months, the state was everything I dreamed it would be. Then the sneezing started. Everything is bigger in Texas, and apparently, that goes for allergy season too. The trees, the grass, even the cockroaches were all out to get me. I was allergic to them all. It was as if the state itself rallied against me to let me know that I was not welcome there. The local allergist and I began a mutually beneficial relationship: he helped me feel better, and my frequent visits probably paid off a good chunk of his children's future college tuition. One day a new symptom popped up. I was itchy; but it wasn't just my eyes or nose this time. It was my entire body. I knew the constant scratching would eventually drive me insane if I didn't find a solution, so I made another appointment.

When my allergist looked me over, he asked some basic questions. Had I recently been exposed to anything unusual or traveled to a foreign country? "No," I responded. He then asked me if anything new was happening in my life. I informed him that I was starting to travel more often for work. Also, we unexpectedly found out we were expecting baby number four, stirring up excitement, but also gnawing concerns that we were quickly outgrowing our small suburban home. Further, my wife just stopped working to spend more time at the house, so money was tight. And on top of it all, I had recently turned thirty, which sent all sorts of existential questions coursing through my mind. These worries flowed out of me like a fire hose on full blast. The doctor eventually cut me off mid-sentence and informed me that the hives were not an allergy but were caused by my anxiety.

At that moment, I realized just what anxiety can do to a person. Unfortunately, though it was the first time my body physically reacted to stress, it wasn't the last. Like many people, I grapple with restless nights, irritability, and even mild bouts of depression amid the pressures of life. Many of us battle with stress caused by an angst-filled mind, constant pressures to perform, and the fear that happiness will always be just out of reach. As our anxiety grows, fear and trepidation take root deep within our hearts and souls. Small frustrations become like giant mountains blocking our path to inner peace. When stress piles up, we quickly become transfixed on our anxieties instead of transformed by our hope.

Acknowledging Angst

Discovering the roots of our anxiety can be difficult. Some of us, for instance, feel completely overwhelmed when we look at our to-do lists; the checklist is too long, and the expectations too high. Others fear they don't have any specific direction for their lives, let alone their day, which incites panic. Or for some, the cause of anxiety can be more nebulous. Maybe they feel like something is about to go wrong any minute now, and they can do nothing about it. Just looking at social media inundates us with details of our friends' lives, the good and bad, as well as all the problems around the world. With the deluge of unnecessary information and negativity to which we are exposed every day, it's incredible we aren't dissolving into a puddle of tears more often.

Everyone's experience with anxiety is unique. What causes angst within one person will not necessarily affect someone else in the same way. Though anxiety is unique, it is not unusual. In today's world, anxiety is an epidemic that affects young and old alike. One study found that the average teen today has the same level of anxiety as a mental health patient from the 1950s.[2] This level of stress is dangerous because it can push us into behaviors and situations that are not only destructive but sinful. Afraid to be alone, many young people jump into unhealthy relationships. Or, driven by a fear of failure, students cheat on tests and exams. And tragically, many teens and adults succumb to self-harm and other dangerous practices as an escape from the internal torment that weighs so heavily on their hearts and suffocates their hope.

Ignoring our internal angst is like not attending to an open wound. Our anxiety causes more problems when it's allowed to fester. To address the root of anxiety and not just the symptoms, we must get to the source of our interior aches and pains. This can be difficult. Emotional pain is much more challenging to address than physical pain. We instinctively avoid and respond to physical pain. For example, if we have a bruise on our leg, we typically don't push on it because we know it will hurt. Or, if we place our hand on something hot, we immediately pull it quickly back to safety. Though the effects of emotional pain and anxiety can be just as damaging, many of us aren't as hasty to react.

We need to be able to acknowledge that something is off. Here we discover the first step to regaining our hope and releasing our anxiety. Then, sometimes with the help of a professional, we have to be willing to dig below the surface of life's busyness to take an in-depth look at what is behind our anxiety. Taking a moment to reflect, pray, and breathe can sometimes be enough to alleviate our anxiety. It is important to note, however, that God is not beyond using friends, family, counselors, and in some cases medicine to bring healing. Some of us may need to seek a listening ear or professional who can help us reach the deep roots of our anxiety and rediscover hope. Even if our struggles with stress and anxious feelings never end, it's still possible to hope in Christ. But we must also be willing to go beyond ourselves for answers. Only Jesus is our ultimate hope for relief and restoration.

Cast Our Anxiety on God

When he inspired the Scriptures, God knew that worry would be an issue for the human person. For times when our minds race with "what ifs" and other worries, the Bible gives inspired insights and wisdom. Over and over, Scripture speaks directly to the human experience of anxiety. In one of his letters, Peter instructs the young Church, "Cast all your worries upon him because he cares for you." (1 Pt 5:7). Casting our concerns onto God is a powerful image, but it's also a challenging one. We are naturally inclined toward independence and self-sufficiency. Some may view this command as mere metaphor, suggestion, or maybe even exaggeration. Others may think it just doesn't apply to them. But make no mistake: Peter's encouragement is not a nicety, it's a necessity. Peter is describing what should be a standard practice for every follower of Christ. Yet, many of us shoulder our troubles for far too long before giving them over to God.

At the end of the verse, Peter points out a reason why we should cast our concerns onto God: "because he cares for you" (1 Pt 5:7). God is not blind to our wants and needs. He is a good Father: compassionate, attentive, and loving. God sees us, knows us, and desires our well-being. This crucial part of the verse helps to rid us from restlessness while also harnessing us to hope. When we truly accept the reality of God's care and concern for us, it can change our entire outlook on life. We have a good Father who takes care of us and knows what's best for us.

For example, one of my strengths as a father is my snack-making expertise. I'd like to think I've perfected the art of snacking. One time, I microwaved marshmallows, peanut butter, and chocolate inside stale ice cream cones. My kids thought I was a creative genius. That day, they treated me like royalty. Though I enjoy being the king of snacks, I don't cave to my kids' snacking demands if it will ruin their appetites. I know what's best for them. I don't always give them what they want—but I always give them what they need. As my kids get older, they have begun to understand that truth more and more. If my children have learned to trust their imperfect dad, how much more should we be able to trust our perfect heavenly Father?

God knows and cares about our needs, worries, and concerns. But when the anxieties build up, this can be tough to believe. At worst, they can even cause us to doubt God's existence. Yet, Jesus promised to take care of us. He assures us of this in the Sermon on the Mount:

Therefore I tell you, do not worry about your life, what you will eat [or drink], or about your body, what you will wear. Is not life more than food and the body more than clothing? Look at the birds in the sky; they do not sow or reap, they gather nothing into barns, yet your heavenly Father feeds them. Are not you more important than they? Can any of you by worrying add a single moment to your life-span? Why are you anxious about clothes? Learn from the way the wild flowers grow. They do not work or spin. But I tell you that not even Solomon in all his splendor was clothed like one of them. If God so clothes the grass of the field, which grows today and is thrown into the oven tomorrow, will he not much more provide for you, O you of little faith? So do not worry and say, "What are we to eat?" or "What are we to drink?" or "What are we to wear?" All these things the pagans seek. Your heavenly Father knows that you need them all. But seek first the kingdom [of God] and his righteousness, and all these things will be given you besides. Do not worry about tomorrow; tomorrow will take care of itself. (Mt 6:25–40)

If God tends to the shrubbery on the ground and birds in the sky, how much more can we trust that he will tenderly watch over us?

We are God's children made in his very own image and likeness. He cares about every aspect of our lives. Despite knowing this, continually casting our anxieties on God can be a daily struggle. But with God's grace, we can fight to entrust our anxiety to God. The battle is worth it because we hope in a loving God who cares for us. Hope changes the narrative.

Trusting Hope

We must understand that entrusting our anxiety to God is not a one-time thing. If it seems impossible to entrust all our fears and worries to God, we can begin with small steps. First, we can try to trust God with our day. Or, if that's too much, we can trust him with the next ten minutes. After ten minutes are up, we can give him another ten minutes. Then we can work up to twenty or thirty minutes. Over time, we gain more confidence to continually cast all our anxieties upon him. Eventually, doing so not only becomes easier but also more natural. Giving over our anxiety can become as routine as breathing; this is best accomplished in the context of prayer.

Saint Thomas Aquinas called prayer "an expression of hope." It's an expression of hope because when we pray, we acknowledge God's sovereignty and care for us despite any anxiety. During stressful times, therefore, it helps to silently say a short prayer or a Scripture verse asking God to help us to trust in him. For instance, we could pray, "Jesus, I trust in you" over and over and over again. Or, we could repeat the name of Jesus prayerfully. We can also pray an act of hope, such as the following:

> O my God, relying on your infinite goodness and promises, I hope to obtain pardon of my sins, the help of your grace, and life everlasting, through the merits of Jesus Christ, my Lord and Redeemer.[3]

Over time, our prayer might even help us to see anxiety more positively. Rather than filling us with dread, anxiety can be seen as an opportunity to grow in the virtue of hope because it drives us to God in prayer.

As we practice placing our trust in God in prayer, we discover his trustworthiness. This is important because trust is the key to living an anxiety-free life. Of course, placing trust in someone can be scary. We all have encountered people who have betrayed us. Sometimes a person may seem trustworthy and then suddenly prove him or herself unreliable. God, however, is not like any other person we might meet. God is unchangingly good and perfectly trustworthy. We can always trust God. This doesn't mean it's easy to do so. Trusting God can be difficult because he does not always prevent our suffering. And he doesn't always answer our prayers in exactly the way we want. Trusting God doesn't mean that everything in life is going to play out the way we expect or desire. When we place our hope in God, we trust that he is who he says he is. We believe that God is a good Father who is in control of our lives, even when things feel uncontrollable.

Truth be told, control is an illusion. The idea that we can take care of every aspect of our lives and prevent bad things from happening is simply not true. Some things we cannot change, prevent, or alter. But God holds the whole world in his hands—remember singing that when we were children? If he holds the world in existence, then he's holding you too. It's not easy to entrust our anxiety to God in today's world. Overcoming anxieties may be a never-ending battle. Anxiety, however, is not a failure of faith; it's part of the human condition. We will always have worries, but they don't have to rule over us.

God has promised to take care of us. And when God says something, it means he's going to do it. Will we worry or worship? Will we panic or praise? Will we be led by our fears or by our faith? When life is unnerving, God will give us the grace to choose hope. Our anxieties won't necessarily disappear, but in the midst of them, all we need do is turn our eyes to Christ. God will come through. It may not always be in the ways we want, know, or understand, but he is dependable, good, and never-changing. We can rest in his ironclad promises. We are not forgotten; we are not on our own. When our hope is in Jesus, we don't have to worry about our worries anymore.

Discussion Questions

1. What are some common situations in your life that trigger anxiety?

2. What is your usual method of coping with stress and angst? Do you think Jesus would suggest something different?

3. How does anxiety hold you back from the hope and confident faith for which you long?

CHAPTER SIX

Hope for the Weary

"Our hearts are restless until they rest in you."[1]

—SAINT AUGUSTINE

I RECENTLY CAME across a study that found only one in seven people wake up feeling refreshed.[2] It caught my attention because I love to sleep. I love sleep so much that I have named my bed Saint Mattress of Comfort. Some people are night people; others are morning people. I'm a sleep person. Sure, I like to stay up late, and my kids ensure I get up early. But, to me, there's nothing more magnificent than a warm, cozy bed in a cold, dark room. Maybe this sounds self-indulgent, but I'm pretty sure it's biblical. After all, Scripture tells us, "It is vain for you to rise early and put off your rest at night, to eat bread earned by hard toil—all this God gives to his beloved in sleep" (Ps 127:2). This might be my favorite verse in the entire Bible.

Like many of us, I often don't get enough sleep. I don't know if the solution to our weariness is simply to get more shut-eye. No matter how many hours we sleep, life can be overwhelmingly busy. Life's burdens and demands can quickly wear us down. We try to pump ourselves up with empty platitudes like "When the going gets tough, the tough get going" or "No pain, no gain." But these clichés don't alleviate our weariness. When it comes to our exhaustion, sometimes the cause is apparent, but often we have no idea why we are so weary. The root cause could be physical, but it could also be mental, emotional, or spiritual. Or, more than likely, it's a combination of some or all of the above.

We've been trained from a young age to keep busy and to seek success. We often don't even realize the pressures we are placing on ourselves. Generally, we think, "If I get good grades in school, I can get a good job. Then when I get a good job, I can make a lot of money. Then when I make a lot of money I can...." At this point our line of thinking often begins to deteriorate. Live in a big house? Retire early? Buy a boat? These things in themselves aren't bad, but they will never be enough to satisfy us. Born to Italian immigrants, Lee Iacocca, an automobile mogul and millionaire business guru, was the perfect example of the American dream. He worked hard and garnered much success and recognition. However, he shared in his autobiography *Talking Straight* that he eventually realized that "fame and fortune is for the birds."[3] Yet we still work end-lessly to be great or successful or famous only to find that in the end, the effort is hardly worth the reward.

Of course, our hard work and a drive for excellence and recognition is not the only cause of our fatigue. Often what really wears us down is our obsessive need to "keep up" with those around us. We don't just want to be great, we want to be greater. We find ourselves constantly com-paring and competing with others. We all know the feeling. That moment when we realize we've taken dozens of self-ies in an attempt to look effortlessly perfect while our friends just seem to roll out of bed looking like models (#jealous). Or, in college, when we've crammed all night for a final and eked out a B and our classmate got a full night's rest and aced the exam. Or when a colleague gets a new car or goes on a dream vacation and, all of a sudden, our life seems monotonous and tiresome.

When we obsessively hone our skills and burn the can-dle at both ends in an attempt to get ahead, we place ourselves in danger of completely burning out. We believe that if we stop to take a breather, we'll fall behind and won't ever be able to make up the difference. So we work, labor, and toil. Eventually, we're caught in a cycle that seems endless and hopeless. Catholic philosopher Josef Pieper warned of this when he wrote,

> The world of work begins to become—threatens to become—our only world, to the exclusion of all else. The demands of the working world grow ever more total, grasping ever more completely the whole of human existence.[4]

But this isn't the world Jesus intended for us. We were created for more. Fortunately, we have a God who understands our weakness and exhaustion and extends hope.

Naps and Snacks

In the Gospel of John, Jesus tells us, "I came so that they might have life and have it more abundantly" (10:10). The problem for many of us, however, is that our lives don't feel abundant. They feel empty even though our calendars are full. Life is so jam-packed with school, sports, extracurricular activities, work, errands, and other commitments that we don't have time for anything else. We're so busy that we don't have time for the things that fill us with joy and give us life—and that's a problem.

One summer, in a seven-week span, I moved across the country, started working at a nonprofit that serves youth in the inner city, bought a house, traveled well over twelve thousand miles, and spoke to roughly fifteen thousand young people about Jesus. During this time, I experienced countless blessings, but my life soon began to feel burdensome. On the one hand, the daily grind kept me distracted from some of the difficulties and angst that naturally come with moving, starting a new job, buying a house, and traveling. On the other hand, I found it incredibly challenging to be present to my loved ones. I was so empty and worn out that I couldn't give quality time or attention to anyone or anything, including my prayer, family, friends, teaching, or ministry. I was frustrated with myself, and I was frustrated and upset with God.

I was willing myself forward, just trying to stay ahead of my calendar, but internally I was a wreck. When I tried to pray, I couldn't hear or feel God in prayer. At times, it felt like I had absolutely nothing left to give. I'd sit down to pray, but afterward, instead of feeling refreshed, I felt more drained. I'd speak to thousands about Jesus and then step off the stage and immediately question everything I had said and shared. Even after witnessing God do some powerful and miraculous things, I'd find myself merely thinking, "I'm tired." I also felt discouraged that so many of my requests and petitions went unanswered by God even while I saw him doing so much for others. Like a car running on empty, I was feeling ineffective and completely depleted.

During this time, I came across a passage about the prophet Elijah that I hadn't read in a while. It's the story of how the prophet encountered God on a mountain (see 1 Kgs 18, 19). To give a speedy summary: Elijah works a significant miracle and defeats an army of false prophets. This upsets his enemy, Queen Jezebel, and she vows revenge. Elijah then freaks out and goes on the run. During the ensuing adventure, the exhausted prophet takes some time to rest:

> [Elijah] lay down and fell asleep under the solitary broom tree, but suddenly a messenger touched him and said, "Get up and eat!" He looked and there at his head was a hearth cake and a jug of water. After he ate and drank, he lay down again, but the angel of the LORD came back a second time, touched him, and said, "Get up and eat or the journey will be too much for you!" He

got up, ate, and drank; then strengthened by that food,
he walked forty days and forty nights to the mountain
of God, Horeb. (1 Kgs 19:5–8)

Elijah was scared and fatigued. He was running for his
life, and how did God minister to him? Elijah took a nap,
and God gave him a meal! Then they repeated the process.
In other words, the Bible reveals that we worship a God of
naps and snacks!

The Church teaches that grace builds upon nature;
God's grace needs a good natural foundation to build on.
As followers of Jesus, we are not only called to take care of
our spiritual lives, but also of our physical health. We cannot separate our spiritual well-being from our physical
well-being—they go together! I think we sometimes forget this; I know I do. I think we all have felt like Elijah. I
felt like him that summer. But reading this passage helped
me to remember that God truly cares about our well-
being, both spiritual and physical. And what happens after
the prophet rests is also significant to remember. The
prophet's nap gave him the energy to be open to an
encounter with God on Mount Horeb. After some crazy
winds, raging fires, and even an earthquake, Elijah encounters God in "a light silent sound" (1 Kgs 19:12). This order
of events can't be a coincidence. The prophet rests and
then, despite some pretty loud distractions, he remarkably
encounters God. This passage shows us that there's a correlation between our ability to rest and our capacity to
experience God.

Rest in Jesus

In the Gospel of Matthew, Jesus tells his disciples, "Come to me, all you who labor and are burdened, and I will give you rest. Take my yoke upon you and learn from me, for I am meek and humble of heart; and you will find rest for yourselves. For my yoke is easy, and my burden light" (11:28–30). I'm guessing many of us have heard this verse before, but when was the last time we paused to dwell on what it truly means? Why, in the face of the world's many problems, does Jesus offer rest? People are hurting. People are dying. Why doesn't Jesus offer solutions? Why doesn't he take away our pain? After all, Jesus came to offer salvation. The world is wallowing in sin, and Jesus simply invites us to rest. Why?

Perhaps we don't fully appreciate Jesus' offer because rest isn't highly valued in the modern world. Keeping busy is practically considered a virtue while rest has become synonymous with laziness. People who make sure they get enough rest aren't generally affirmed in our culture. "Dude, you napped so hard yesterday. Nice!"—said pretty much no one ever. We learn from a young age that busyness is commendable, and some of us don't even really know how to rest.

What kind of rest is Jesus talking about exactly? Is he inviting us to a quiet night with our favorite comfort foods, sweatpants, and binge-worthy television shows? There's nothing wrong with taking some downtime, but before we get too excited, let's be clear. Jesus is offering something much better than a relaxing couple of hours. Christ offers us a lasting rest, peace, and wholeness for our bodies and souls that will permeate every aspect of our lives. While some religions focus on how humans must labor to reach the heights of God, Christianity reveals a God who comes to us. Jesus meets us on our level, in our humanity. Our faith relies not on what we do, but on what Christ has already done. We find rest when we turn to God in prayer and trust that he will help us to move forward with his grace, even when it feels like we aren't moving at all.

God stitched rest into the fabric of creation. After he created the world, God rested on the seventh day. Of course, our omnipresent, omnipotent God didn't get tired after six days of work; that would go against his nature. Instead, God was giving us an example to follow for our good. We weren't created to work constantly. We need rest. The *Catechism of the Catholic Church* teaches, "The institution of the Lord's Day helps everyone enjoy adequate rest and leisure to cultivate their familial, cultural, social, and religious lives" (2184). Adding rest to our schedule might seem like just another thing on our ever-growing to-do list. When we add the right things to our calendars, our days become more invigorating than exhausting. Moments of prayer, time with friends, and even hobbies may sound unproductive when our schedule is packed, but it's usually what we need the most. And, sometimes the most productive (and holy) thing we can do is to rest.

Sometimes when we're feeling exhausted, it's important to note that our pursuit of holy things can wear us down too. Over the years, I have had the honor of witnessing many young people decide to follow Jesus more closely. Sometimes though, the conversations that follow a young person's commitment to Jesus concern me. Some tell me they're going to commit to daily holy hours—as in plural. Or they vow to pray multiple Rosaries before breakfast or fast on bread and water until God tells them to stop. Though their intentions are good and their eagerness contagious, I try to steer them away from such huge spiritual undertakings. These grand gestures of faith aren't necessarily bad, but one also wouldn't recommend a marathon to someone who never exercises. When spiritual practices are undertaken without the help of God's grace and the promptings of the Holy Spirit, they can lead us to weariness and fatigue rather than to joy and peace.

Make no mistake, Jesus does call us to do great things for his kingdom. But our work is most efficacious when it comes from a heart at rest in God. Like a child in the loving arms of a parent, we can find comfort and respite in the Lord. Psalm 62 tells us, "My soul rests in God alone, from whom comes my salvation" (62:2). The natural byproduct of placing our hope in God is rest. With our gaze on God, all that wearies us will be put into perspective. Then, despite the chaos of our calendars, we can always make space for rest.

Balanced by Hope

Though rest is important, a desire to do good, accomplish goals, and to be successful is not necessarily bad. Our drive to do good, when it's in union with God's will, can be a result of the much-forgotten virtue of magnanimity. Saint Thomas Aquinas taught that "magnanimity is chiefly about the hope of something difficult."[5] Magnanimity helps us to stop binge-watching TV or wasting hours a day scrolling on social media and to use that time to serve God and others. Magnanimity pushes us and gives us the courageous hope to do great things for the kingdom of God. We are lacking in magnanimity when we find it difficult to believe that God calls us to do great things. When our drive to do great things for God, however, is more about us than about God, it can push us past our limits and leave us exhausted.

Luckily, another virtue can safeguard our energy and hope: humility. Whereas magnanimity is mostly forgotten, humility is often misunderstood. Far too often, humility is associated with a quiet, self-deprecating disposition that fades into the background so others can take the spotlight. The virtue is less about our relationships with other people and more about our relationship with God. Humility tethers us to the truth that God is God, and we are not. Saint Paul shows us what truthful humility looks like when he proclaims, "But by the grace of God I am what I am, and his grace to me has not been ineffective. Indeed, I have toiled harder than all of them; not I, however, but the grace of God [that is] with me" (1 Cor 15:10). Humility gives Christians the freedom to anchor our hope not in our accomplishments, ego, or reputation but in a loving God.

Josef Pieper once wrote, "Magnanimity and humility are the most essential prerequisites for the preservation and unfolding of supernatural hope."[6] Magnanimity and humility help us to maintain and grow in hope; the former pushes us to hope in all the great things God has planned for us, while the latter helps us to see that God is far greater than any accolades we might receive. When we find ourselves balanced in these virtues, we will find that our lives become more balanced as well. When we anchor our hope in God, and not in our skillsets or accomplishments, we can rest knowing that God will provide. And we find freedom knowing that God is in control of this crazy world, not us.

Finding balance and rest is an ongoing challenge in our busy world. But when we lean into a rhythm of rest, we will more easily respond to God's grace, which allows us to be more fruitful in our work. We also can trust that God will give us the grace and resources needed to structure our lifestyle in a way that lends itself to our spiritual growth. Hope empowers us to balance our calendars with activities that replenish and allow us to thrive. Placing our hope in God means we allow him to do the heavy lifting and trust in his grace to carry us through any fatigue we might experience in doing his will. If we are tired and worn out and find that our schedule is imbalanced, we can rest assured that we are being invited to rest with our God of naps and snacks.

Discussion Questions

1. Have you ever been too busy for your own good? How did you address the stress and weariness you were experiencing?

2. When you are driven to be busy, even at the cost of your own well-being, what do you think you are hoping in rather than God?

3. What are some things you can schedule into your week that will help you to recharge and remain focused on Jesus?

CHAPTER SEVEN

Hope for the Addict

"For freedom Christ set us free."

—GALATIANS 5:1

MARK JI TIANXIANG was a successful and well-respected doctor who lived in nineteenth-century China. A pious Catholic who often did pro bono work for those who could not afford medical care, Ji became addicted to opioids after innocently using it to treat himself for a stomach illness. Though he understood little about addiction, he never gave up the fight for freedom. He visited the sacrament of Reconciliation often until his confessor, who also did not understand that addiction is a disease, told him to cease receiving the sacraments because he thought

Ji simply did not have the resolve to change his ways. For thirty years, Ji obediently abstained from the Eucharist and from confession. But he never left the Church. He persevered in prayer and continued to lean into God's love for him. When the Boxer Rebellion began in 1900, Christian persecution broke out across China. Along with his entire family, Ji was arrested and taken into custody. Even while imprisoned, his addiction impelled him to continue to use opium. Eventually, Ji was executed and died singing a litany to the Blessed Virgin Mary. On October 1, 2000, Mark Ji Tianxiang was officially canonized a saint by the Church. A man who actually died an active addict was made a saint.

Saint Mark Ji Tianxiang knew all too well that few things can seem as truly hopeless as addiction. One does not have to struggle personally with addiction to enter into the hopelessness that it can cause. Addiction is everywhere, and it's an easy path to despair. I've seen the effects of addiction up close through my work at a Catholic nonprofit that serves youth in inner-city neighborhoods. It is not uncommon for kids to be left to fend for themselves while their Mom goes on a bender. Dad is absent or jumps from job to job because of his addiction. Some have even witnessed deaths due to overdose within the walls of their own homes. Though addiction is less hidden in the inner city, the same use and abuse exists in the most well-off and seemingly pleasant suburbs. From the rich to the impoverished, addiction runs rampant. It does not discriminate. Through all socioeconomic statuses, levels of education, races, gender, and religions, it's hard to find an individual who hasn't been affected by a disease of dependency.

When we face problems related to addiction, either personally or with a loved one, everything can appear to be hopeless. But amid these struggles, we too can strive for sainthood. Saint Mark Ji Tianxiang is an example of someone who continued to be faithful to God, despite his addiction. Today, more than in Ji's day, education about the disease of addiction is prevalent, and many more resources are available to help addicts. Addiction truly can be overcome with the spiritual aid of the sacraments and the help of encouraging friends, family, support groups, and medical professionals. Whether or not we personally wrestle with addiction, we can remain rooted in hope—for ourselves and for our loved ones. We have hope because we know that God is a liberator, and he wants to set us free.

Assessing Addiction

Addiction is a complex disease involving genetics, life experiences, and brain circuits in which a person compulsively engages in the chronic use of substances or certain behaviors, despite their negative consequences. Most medical professionals classify addiction as a disease because it changes brain structure and function in a way that makes a person's desire for something all-consuming. Addiction is insidious in that few realize it is taking hold. No one plans to become an addict. What can start in the pursuit of pleasure or as a needed distraction from the concerns of the world, can soon turn into a life of never-ending dependency, a never-satiated ache. At the same time, addicts often build up a tolerance to the substance, which means they need more to obtain the buzz or high they crave. All this creates a brutal cycle difficult to break.

Life-threatening substance abuse may not be a part of our personal stories. Addiction, however, is not something that merely waits at the bottom of a bottle or the end of a needle. From shopping or eating, sex and pornography, screens and entertainment, dependency and addiction take many shapes and forms. The reality is that each of us could be one bad decision away from the start of an addiction. A seemingly harmless habit can quickly progress into a disease that hijacks our brains, causing a craving so fierce that it dictates our behavior despite our knowledge of the adverse consequences. Even if we ourselves have escaped a struggle with addiction, chances are we know people who are feeling trapped in a destructive cycle. Whether or not our bad habits or sins ever rise to the level of addiction, we can always identify areas where God's grace, and in some cases professional help, is needed.

Today, many men and women find themselves enslaved to pornography. Tens of millions of people report visiting pornographic sites regularly. Though society often dismisses the danger of viewing pornography, a study found that brain scans of individuals viewing pornography were eerily similar to those of cocaine addicts.[1] Unfortunately, with smart phones, the temptation to online pornography can be incessant. For those who struggle with pornography, having a phone in one's pocket is like an alcoholic walking around with a free drink coupon to the local bar. But it isn't just sexual sins that can lead to compulsive behavior.

According to some studies, 5 to 10 percent of people in the United States meet the requirements necessary to be classified as addicted to social media.[2] For those who hate math, that's somewhere around 32 million people. Other studies claim the number of social media addicts in the United States could actually be a staggering 38 percent, or 124 million people![3] Whether or not we're addicted to social media, if we are honest, chances are most of us use it a bit too much. Most people rise and shine by scrolling through their social media feeds. And, a recent study declared that the average millennial will take over twenty-five thousand selfies in his or her lifetime.[4] Now, the internet isn't bad in itself, but when it leads us to crave online likes more than real human contact and love—that's a major problem.

The list of addictions and potentially addictive behaviors goes on and on. Food is a basic necessity for human survival, but some use it to escape from reality. Others use shopping similarly. When life is too much, some turn to compulsive buying. Just the phrase "retail therapy," which we use in jest, acknowledges an underlying issue. Gambling. Gaming. Tobacco. Adrenaline junkies. Addiction is so rampant that hundreds of billions of dollars are spent every year to offset the health care cost, crime, and lost economic productivity. But the loss of economic productivity is not nearly as costly as the loss of hope.

Breaking Free

In the Acts of the Apostles, Paul and Silas perform an exorcism on a female slave. One might think that would be cause for celebration, but the livid slave owner instead had the two men severely beaten and thrown in jail. Now, if this happened to me, I would classify that day as pretty lousy. But Paul and Silas don't curl up in the corner of their prison cell and feel sorry for themselves. Instead, they spend their time singing praises to God. Maybe this is how we expect biblical characters to behave, but to me, their reaction seems a bit outlandish. Let's recap the facts: Paul and Silas are in jail. They are shackled in a dark and dank room, bloodied and bruised from an unjust beating. There's no escape. Their future is unknown and entirely out of their control. Hope should seem lost. Yet, it isn't.

As Paul and Silas sing into the night, an earthquake suddenly occurs. Earthquakes usually cause death and destruction, but this one does the opposite. As the jail trembles, the doors fly open, and the prisoners' chains and bonds come loose. Miraculously, God's power breaks in, and Paul and Silas are set free. One wonders what their reactions were like in that moment. Did the earthquake scare them senseless? Were they surprised that freedom had come to them in a single instant? We may never know, but I have a strong suspicion that Paul knew everything was going to be just fine from the start.

Now, God doesn't work a miracle in our lives every time we need one. Paul and Silas knew that. In fact, they may have been resigned to the possibility of spending the remainder of their days in a dirty jail cell. But they still had hope, regardless of the outcome. They had hope because, despite their chains, they were already free men. As Paul wrote to the Galatians, "For freedom Christ set us free; so stand firm and do not submit again to the yoke of slavery" (5:1). In Jesus we can find freedom from any sinful habit and from the chains of addiction. Paul and Silas fully accepted the Gospel message, so no matter their circumstances, they knew that their freedom was in Christ.

That same freedom has been extended to all of us. Do we know that? I once read how baby elephants in the circus are trained. To the dismay of animal rights activists, baby elephants are shackled or tied to a stake in the ground. If the elephant tries to wander away, it is stopped by the restraints. Despite their attempts to break free, the elephants soon realize all efforts are futile. As the elephants grow bigger and stronger, they are soon physically capable of breaking free. But the trainers never change the restraints. Because of the elephants' past experiences, they don't even try to escape; they believe their efforts are futile and their situation hopeless.

Perhaps we think that this elephant analogy does not apply to our lives or our problems. Like a chained elephant, we may think we're not strong enough to break free from sinful habits and certainly not from addiction. In a certain sense, that's correct; we aren't strong enough on our own. But our hope is not in ourselves; it's in God who dwells within us. Though we are often weaker than we want to admit, our God is stronger than we can imagine. As Saint Paul said, "My grace is sufficient for you, for power is made perfect in weakness" (2 Cor 12:9). By virtue of our Baptism, the same power that conquered the grave dwells in us. And if God can defeat death, he can defeat our bad habits and even our addictions. We are not meant to be enslaved. God wants us and our loved ones to seek the spiritual and professional help necessary to break free from the chains of addiction. The shackles that bind us can and must be broken.

Hope and Holy Friendships

For the addict, freedom might sound inaccessible and impossible. But nothing is impossible with God. Perhaps God will shake our world like an earthquake, and the fetters of addiction will fall in an instant. But it's more likely that he'll move subtly, helping us to find the professional help and support groups that will lead us to understand the underlying reasons for our compulsive behavior. The disease of addiction takes hold over time, so it often takes time to be fully liberated. Either way, by God's grace, the yoke of slavery placed on us by addiction can be removed. Hope is always possible.

In college, a buddy told me a story about a young man that will forever remain in my memory. My friend shared with me that during a men's retreat that he was leading, a young man spoke up. The teen bravely shared about his battle with a pornography addiction with the other young men. In his efforts to stop viewing pornography, the young man put his computer in the family room because it had become too big a temptation in his bedroom. He thought the added foot traffic would keep him from feeding his habit. But he still succumbed to temptation. So he moved his computer again, this time to the kitchen. But he continued to view pornography.

In a moment of desperation (or maybe inspiration), the young man decided to do something more decisive. When he was home alone, he got down on all fours and chewed through the family's ethernet cable. The best part? He blamed the family dog for the severed cable. Now, I don't condone lying, but I do admire that young man's resolve. He was not complacent, and he knew things had to radically change. He cooperated with God's grace and did all he could do to avoid temptation. But what was even more powerful than breaking his internet connection was sharing his struggle with people around him who could provide encouragement, support, and accountability. It must have been embarrassing for him to share his problems with pornography with the group, but in doing so he acknowledged that our battles are not meant to be fought alone.

We are social creatures. We are made in the image and likeness of God, and God is a community of persons— Father, Son, and Spirit. So we too need community. We are made for one another. We are made to show one another love and support. And we are not meant to only share the happy moments with others but also the difficult ones. This is especially true when facing something as severe as addiction. The stigma around addiction or sinful habits can lead us to hide our problematic behaviors from others. In moments of dejection, we might isolate ourselves from others because we think no one else would understand our plight or offer help. But in doing so, we place ourselves in a position where addiction can continue to run rampant. Isolation makes the fight against addiction exponentially more difficult. Many people find freedom from addiction by surrounding themselves with a supportive community, whether through support groups, medical professionals, spiritual directors, church friends, family, or all of the above. As we close this chapter, we'll focus on just one helpful relationship that can help us to avoid addiction—friendship.

The Book of Sirach reminds us, "Faithful friends are a sturdy shelter; whoever finds one finds a treasure" (6:14). Confiding in a friend can pull us out of darkness and back into the light. When sharing with a trusted, wise friend, we often find that they have had similar experiences and can give us insights and solutions that bring comfort. Sometimes their journey can open our eyes to see hope again. And even if that isn't the case, when we turn to a friend, at least we have someone to weather the storm with us. A good friend won't be able to beat our addiction for us, but they can be there to help shoulder the burden, and that can make a world of difference.

Even if we are not facing an addiction or vice, we all need holy friendships that point and repoint us to the object of our hope—God. We all would do well to ask ourselves, "Who can I lean on when facing difficulties?" "Do my friends point me to God? When was the last time I opened up and was vulnerable with a friend?" If we don't have answers to these questions, it's time to seek these types of relationships and opportunities. And if we don't have a supportive, faithful friend, we can ask God to provide someone. We all need friends who keep us accountable and to pick us up when we stumble. God wants us to have people like this in our lives. We may feel like hope is lost but good, faithful friends can remind us that freedom in Christ is possible.

Our addictions and bad habits may be strong, but God is always stronger. We may feel like hope has been lost, but freedom is possible in Christ. When we move toward healing, we must keep in mind that freedom is not free. The good news is that the cross of Christ has already paid the cost. But we still need to cooperate in God's grace. When fighting addiction, we cannot be passive in our healing process. Though it may be an uphill climb, God will give us the grace to climb the steep steps toward healing. At times it may feel like we are running. At other times walking. Or maybe it will feel more like a slow army crawl through the muck. The important thing is that we continue to move forward in hope. Our vices can be vanquished. Our addictions conquered. God is there even in our dependencies and addiction, and no bottle or drug or screen can change that. Even for the addict, there is hope.

Discussion Questions

1. What is a habit or vice you have that is or has the potential to become problematic?

2. What are some ways you can assist addicts, whether friends, family, or people in your church and local community?

3. What are some friendships in your life that help you to hold onto hope even when you feel like things are hopeless?

CHAPTER EIGHT

Hope for the Suffering

"I wish to suffer for Love's sake, and for Love's sake even to rejoice. This is how I scatter flowers."[1]

—Saint Thérèse of Lisieux

A FEW YEARS ago, near Thanksgiving, I started to notice tingling in my hands and feet; it felt like my limbs were falling asleep, only it hurt. At first, I brushed it off, not thinking much of it. But next came a numbness in various parts of my body. Menial tasks, such as climbing stairs, became difficult and dangerous. Soon, fatigue completely overwhelmed my waking hours. Some days I found it almost impossible to get out of bed. Then I started to experience muscle twitching, memory problems, chest pains, and heart palpitations. Insomnia and depression followed shortly after. (And those were just *some* of my symptoms. I will spare you the unpleasant details of the others!) Apparently out of nowhere, it suddenly seemed as if my body was shutting down. Little did I know that the suffering was just beginning.

As my symptoms continued to worsen, I spent the next eight months making countless visits to doctors, specialists, and hospitals. I was put through a litany of medical tests. I was scanned and x-rayed too many times to count. I was poked and prodded so much that I began to feel more like a human pincushion than a patient. I was tested for cancer, Lou Gehrig's Disease, multiple sclerosis, and a multitude of other illnesses. After months of no answers, a doctor finally diagnosed the underlying cause of my growing list of disturbing symptoms: Lyme disease. Contracted through tick bites, Lyme disease is a strange illness that can manifest itself in various ways. If caught early, it's highly treatable. I wasn't so fortunate.

Before Lyme disease, I didn't think of myself as invincible, but I also didn't realize I was so fragile. I had been through difficult situations before, but nothing matched the pain, both physical and psychological, that I endured with this unexpected illness. Especially in the early months, I felt at moments that I had nothing: no answers, no control, and no direction moving forward. Additionally, most of my symptoms were invisible to the outside world. On the one hand, this saved me from unwanted pity and repetitive conversations. But on the other hand, others could not see what I was going through, which made the experience incredibly isolating. My illness also led me to wrestle with all sorts of unsettling questions. I wondered, "What will happen to my wife and kids if I can't walk or provide or worse? What is my value if this illness is chronic, and I'm unable to work? If my doctors who I can hear, see, and touch can't heal me, how can I trust an invisible God to take care of me? Why would God allow this to happen?"

I don't share my plight to make anyone feel sorry for me. I'm also well aware that others have experienced far greater suffering. Everyone's life story is distinct. Yet inevitably, we all experience pain, stress, and heartbreak. It's the cost of being human. While we may experience suffering to varying degrees and in different ways, no one gets a free pass. It's a simple fact. Suffering is a common denominator for everyone. Maybe some of us haven't experienced really terrible suffering yet. Perhaps some of us may have dodged the bullet of affliction thus far. That isn't a bad thing—but it won't last forever. Others may already know the agony of great suffering. We have walked through times that have taken the air from our lungs and drained the color from our world. Hardships of this kind are inevitable. But hope is possible, even amid the worst kinds of suffering.

Cross Examined

Have you ever thought about the fact that the cross, an instrument of suffering and death, is the central image of our faith? We easily can become a bit desensitized to this reality. Imagine walking into a church and seeing an electric chair or a noose hanging from the ceiling. That would be pretty weird. Yet every Sunday, millions of people gather in spaces where a cross is on prominent display. Nonetheless, we still can easily sanitize the true meaning of the cross and forget about its significance. We've all seen enchanting and even picturesque images of Christ on the cross that don't capture its true reality. Crucifixion was humiliating, agonizing, and horrific. One thing it wasn't was efficient—and that was intentional. The Romans' goal wasn't merely to kill their victims but to mercilessly torment them as a deterrent to any passersby tempted to commit a similar crime. Crucifixion was so awful that Roman citizens were excluded from dying such a cruel death. The word "excruciating" literally means "from the cross." The pain was so intense that a new word was created to describe it.

Think about it for a minute. *This* is how God chose to redeem us—from the cross. Our sovereign, all-powerful, all-mighty God chose to save us through suffering. Without losing his divine nature, the Son of God was sent by the Father to become incarnate and to endure death by crucifixion. In doing so, Jesus took the curse of suffering and death that had entered the world through sin and transformed it into a pathway to salvation. Jesus offered himself as a free and willing victim so that we could become victors. But he did not suffer so that we never would. Instead, Jesus invites us to unite our suffering with his suffering. Some of us like to skip over this part of the Gospel, but Jesus very clearly said that if we want to follow him then we must pick up our crosses and follow him to

Calvary (see Lk 9:23). As Christ embraced his cross, he calls us to do the same. Because of Christ, what was once a symbol of death has now become a symbol of hope.

Boasting of Suffering

In the midst of suffering, however, it can be hard to hold onto hope. A few years ago, I had the privilege of journeying with a friend as he fought cancer. I was living in Houston at the time, and my friend lived four hours away in a smaller city. Due to the superior hospitals and doctors in Houston, he decided to make the trek for his chemotherapy. Every time he was in town, I would do my best to clear my schedule so I could sit with him through his treatments. Even though my friend was very sick, he could still sweet-talk the stripes off a candy cane. He exuded positivity and charm throughout his treatments; the nurses and doctors loved him. But knowing him well, I could tell that despite his optimism, the cancer was taking a toll. Though always kind and light-hearted when someone would come into the room, when it was just us, he would shrink back, becoming somber.

As the weeks dragged into months, my friends' eyes began to show his exhaustion. One time I was with my friend when his treatment ended early. His wife was out running errands, so I offered to take him out for a bite to eat. The only food he could keep down at the time was smoothies; luckily, a Panera Bread was right around the corner. (I know Panera is known for their bread, but their smoothies are grossly underrated. It's a travesty really.) At the restaurant, my friend was reflective, and I could tell something was on his mind. I didn't want to pry, but he must have sensed my concern.

"Do you want to know what I'm thinking?" he said quietly.

My friend didn't wait for me to answer.

"I thought it would be different," he sighed.

I didn't understand what he meant, but he continued.

"I've seen friends and family members struggle. I've seen them endure strokes and heart attacks. I've seen people face seemingly insurmountable odds and hardships. And it seemed like it made them better, more like Jesus. I don't feel like my suffering is doing that."

It was a heartbreaking confession. My friend's pale skin and hairless head revealed the ravages of the disease on his body, but he was giving me a glimpse into his soul. Soon my friend's wife arrived. As they started their journey home, I found myself just sitting in the parking lot, haunted by my friend's words. Though I wasn't experiencing what my friend was, I knew how challenging it can be to remain hopeful while suffering. Thankfully, my friend can now describe how he experienced grace in his past suffering. But sometimes this supernatural view can seem impossible in the moment.

Some people grow closer to God through severe suffering and loss. For others, ache and affliction negatively impact their relationship with God. Still others try to ignore the reality of suffering altogether. For them, suffering is a hindrance and a nuisance; they have a plan and an agenda, and absolutely no time to spare for sprained ankles or broken hearts. Saint Paul shows us how Christians are called to suffer in the Letter to the Romans:

> We boast in hope of the glory of God. Not only that, but we even boast of our afflictions, knowing that affliction produces endurance, and endurance, proven character, and proven character, hope, and hope does not disappoint, because the love of God has been poured out into our hearts through the holy Spirit that has been given to us. (5:2–5)

Paul's rich words speak directly to the hope available to us in and through suffering. Make no mistake, the Apostle knew suffering. During his ministry, Paul endured stoning, lashings, beatings, and being shipwrecked. Then he was imprisoned and martyred. Knowing what Paul endured, one naturally wonders where he got his confidence. For most of us, suffering is something we complain about. How could Paul boast of his afflictions? He speaks of the endurance and character that suffering in Christ can bring forth. Paul holds a hope that doesn't disappoint, no matter how dire the circumstances.

The source of Paul's, and every Christian's, hope in the face of suffering is the cross of Christ. The cross offers an answer to suffering that no other religion or ideology can provide. Some Eastern religions teach that it's possible to free ourselves from pain by freeing ourselves from all our attachments—good or bad. Islam views suffering as a harsh test of faith. Atheists often can only see suffering as a meaningless experience in a meaningless world. Yet, Christ's cross gives us a completely different lens to view suffering. Jesus chose to suffer and die for us, and so we now have a companion in our suffering and not only a companion but a God who can transform our suffering from something meaningful.

Saint Augustine affirmed this profound reality when he wrote, "All those who belong to Jesus Christ are fastened with him to the Cross."[2] In Baptism, when we are plunged into water, we are symbolically being buried in the death of Christ before we rise as a new creation (see *CCC* 1214). This mystery makes it possible for us to unite our sufferings to those of Jesus. In this manner, we actually participate, in some mysterious way, in the redemption of the world. In addition, when we join our pain to the cross, we become more like Jesus. Our suffering is not wasted when it's united to Christ. Thus, afflictions become an unavoidable avenue of grace for all who wish to follow Jesus. This union with Christ on the cross is a source of hope.

The idea of accepting, embracing, and even boasting of our suffering is countercultural. Some even argue it's unchristian. Over the last few decades, the message of the Gospel has been polluted by preachers who promise prosperity and good fortune to anyone who follows Jesus. The mere existence of this type of theology proves just how difficult it can be for us to accept suffering. But Christ spoke quite clearly about the inevitable suffering his followers would experience. One can sympathize, however, with those who want to believe that discipleship leads only to good things. Health and wealth sound great, especially when we don't have it. Yet, we should never ignore the reality of the cross. Even if we do, it doesn't save us from suffering and the painful realities of this world.

Through suffering, God bestowed love and mercy on the world. Precisely because Christ defeated death through suffering, we can have hope when we suffer too. And, like Paul, we too can even boast of our suffering. Since it was through suffering that God chose to save us and bring forth new life, our suffering can be a source of God's grace, even in the worst of circumstances.

Finding Meaning in Misery

Suffering is repulsive in many ways, but united to Christ's passion and death, suffering becomes redemptive. The fancy phrase for uniting our miseries to the cross is "redemptive suffering." This reality is precisely what makes the Christian perspective on suffering so unique. If there were no redeeming value in suffering, then it should be avoided at all costs. Yet, for the believer, suffering can be embraced. Whether it be cancer, slander, or scraped knees, any and every hardship can be united to Christ's cross. When we unite our suffering to Jesus', we participate in his salvific grace, and we grow in hope. Holocaust survivor Viktor Frankl once argued that suffering can actually cease being suffering if a person finds some kind of meaning in it, by making it a sacrifice.[3]

Though offering up our suffering as a sacrifice for others won't actually stop our suffering, it does provide a purpose for our pain and can give us hope in the midst of despair. This idea might be easier to grasp using an analogy. When we lift weights, the repetitive movements tear down the muscle fibers in our bodies. Yet, we endure the

pain and discomfort because we know our muscles will
be repaired, and they will become bigger and stronger
than before. We endure the pain of the workout because
we know that good will come from the struggle. The
same is true in our suffering. Saint Vincent de Paul
understood this well when he taught, "If we could but
know what a precious treasure lies concealed in infirmi-
ties, we would receive them with as much joy as we would
the greatest benefits, and we would bear them without
complaint or any sign of annoyance."[4] When we can find
the meaning in our misery, it makes pain much more
endurable.

Though the aches and pains of lifting weights cannot
compare to true suffering, the rewards of redemptive suffering are so much greater. Saint Paul describes these
rewards in his Second Letter to the Corinthians:

> Although our outer self is wasting away, our inner self is
> being renewed day by day. For this momentary light
> affliction is producing for us an eternal weight of glory
> beyond all comparison, as we look not to what is seen
> but to what is unseen; for what is seen is transitory, but
> what is unseen is eternal. (4:16–18)

The hope of eternal glory outweighs every hurt and
pain found in this world. As hope propels our hearts and
minds to focus on a heavenly future without suffering,
graces come cascading into our current predicaments. We
may not always understand our suffering, but the anchor
of our hope must remain firmly fastened to Christ. We can
be confident that he will use our pain for his purposes.

Following Christ is to embrace pain. But let's be clear, Christians do not glorify suffering. We are not called to be holy masochists. If there's a solution to our suffering, we are free to take it. But when our suffering is inescapable, hope can grant us the grace-filled grit to persevere, endure, redeem, and even boast of our afflictions. Rather than feeling defeated, burdened, or embittered by our pain, the cross helps us to stand confidently as we lean into the transformative and redemptive realities of suffering.

Some of you might be curious to know how I'm doing with Lyme disease. The short answer is that I'm doing better than I was a few years ago. The longer answer is that I still have quite a few bad days. Many of my symptoms have lessened, but I still deal with them daily. It's unlikely I will ever regain the health I once had. And although every ounce of me wishes I was free of this disease, I don't think I would change these past few years. God has been present to me in the suffering in ways I've never experienced him before. This affliction has made me physically weaker but spiritually stronger. Don't get me wrong: I'm not done fighting this disease. Maybe someday I will beat it, but my hope is not in health, medicine, or good doctors. If it were, I would be disappointed. And hope never disappoints. My hope is in Jesus, so this illness is nothing that the resurrection can't cure.

In this world, life doesn't always lead to the happy ending we desire. Some of our stories of suffering won't conclude with joy and relief. But Christian hope never disappoints. Our hardships can either demoralize us or sanctify us. When we accept suffering and unite it to the cross, our lives can truly change as we are made holier by our union with Christ. Amid suffering, by God's grace, may we avoid becoming bitter and allow it to make us better!

Discussion Questions

1. Recall a time you suffered. What helped you endure the pain?

2. How does the Christian view of suffering differ from that of today's culture?

3. What are some prayer practices that help you to remain hopeful in the midst of suffering?

CHAPTER NINE

Hope for the Grieving

"Blessed are those who mourn, for they will be comforted."
—Matthew 5:4

LATE-NIGHT TELEVISION HOSTS lift our spirits and provide entertainment with jokes and funny anecdotes. If they drift from this formula, it's usually considered poor television. An exception to the rule occurred when comedian and late-night television host Stephen Colbert sat down with journalist Anderson Cooper to discuss death, loss, and grief. Their conversation went viral overnight. People found something mesmerizing about the two grown men articulating their thoughts around the universal human experience of suffering and death. Though

Colbert is a comedian, his insights weren't funny as much as they were personal, authentic, and insightful.

Born and raised Catholic, Colbert lost his father and two brothers in a plane crash when he was a child. Cooper also lost his father when he was a boy, and at the time of the interview he was processing the recent death of his mother. In an incredibly raw and touching moment, Anderson Cooper read a quote from Colbert in which he had expressed that he had come to love exactly those things in his life that he wished never happened. Cooper was obviously moved but also incredulous, especially when he recalls Colbert's sentiment that the "punishments" of God can also be seen as gifts. Through tears, he asks Colbert if he really believes what he had said, and Colbert affirmed that he truly does feel this way.

Most of us can probably relate to Anderson Cooper's difficulty believing that severe loss can be a gift. How could anyone say he loves what he most wished never happened? How does anyone accept hurt and loss as a gift from God? Often, nothing about grief, and especially death, feels like a gift. Of course, we also experience grief and loss as a result of a variety of other circumstances: a falling out with a friend, a breakup, divorce, or the loss of a job. Even losing a prized or cherished possession can cause us to grieve. Nevertheless, we experience a special grief when dealing with the permanence of death; it brings a separation that can't be undone this side of heaven. After losing a friend or family member, we enter a time of bereavement, which literally means "to be deprived by death."

Nothing seems to contradict hope more than death. Death is one of life's most traumatic events and can cause significant emotional stress. Grieving the loss of a loved one can make life feel like hell. Those who have mourned a death know this all too well. More than any other time in our life, death challenges hope and potentially leads us to despair. But if we truly desire hope, we must not ignore the reality of man's mortality. We believe that in the face of death and grief, hope still can be found because of the death and resurrection of Jesus Christ.

Death's Devastation

After thousands of years of humankind dealing with grief, one would think that some sort of social, cultural, or even biological response to death would have been discovered to protect us from its sting. Why does death hurt so deeply? It isn't like it's an uncommon occurrence. No one makes it out of this world alive, right? We all know this. Each and every person will die. But we still try to ignore or hide from death. And even if we have accepted the concept of death to some extent, experiencing the reality of a loved ones' passing is another thing all together.

The Book of Wisdom tells us, "God did not make death" (1:13). Death was never part of God's plan for humanity but only entered our world as a result of sin. Therefore, dying is foreign to the very fabric of our being. Yet, we are helpless against it, and perhaps that's why death can make us feel so hopeless. No matter how prepared we feel to say goodbye, loss cuts deep. Boxing champion Mike Tyson once famously said, "Everyone has a plan until they get punched in the mouth." Grieving a death can leave us feeling like we just got knocked out. It's overwhelming, whether or not a person dies peacefully in old age or unexpectedly. The grieving process, however, can be more complicated and devastating when someone dies suddenly. Further still, it can be outright traumatic in cases of suicide.

Tragically, as some of us know all too well, suicide has become more common. Rates in the United States are the highest they've been since World War II. One study showed that across every demographic, suicides have risen by 28 percent over the past two decades.[1] According to the Center for Disease Control, taking one's own life is now the tenth most common cause of death in the country. Worldwide, one person dies from suicide every 40 seconds.[2] It's easy to distance ourselves from these numbers until suicide touches our own lives.

Every year in my ministry I meet people who are grieving the suicide of a loved one or are contemplating the possibility of taking their own life. It isn't just teens and young adults. At the first parish where I served as a youth minister, a grade-school child took her own life to escape the bullying she had been experiencing daily. I've worked with teens whose parents attempted suicide, leaving their family in complete shock and disarray. I've listened as those left behind shared their struggles and tried to comprehend the sudden loss of a loved one. It's incredibly painful and difficult to understand why someone has taken his or her own life. But one thing I've learned from sitting and talking with people in the wake of suicide is that taking one's own life doesn't end the suffering. It simply transfers the pain to those left behind.

Saint Thomas Aquinas taught, "When hope is given up, men rush headlong into sin, and are drawn away from good works."[3] For this reason, despair is one of the most dangerous sins because it causes us to drift away from the life God offers toward the darkness of the grave. Suicide could be accurately labeled "death by despair." Choosing to commit suicide is a serious offense against God and our loved ones. This leads some to insist that those who commit suicide will be damned for eternity. While we must understand the severity of suicide, it's God's job to judge souls. Only God can know a person's heart, and whether he or she truly understood the gravity of the choice. We also can't know what happens in a person's last moments before death; perhaps there was repentance or a short prayer asking for God's forgiveness. Regardless, we entrust all those who have died, whether peacefully or tragically, to God. We know his mercy is far greater than the most egregious sins. Our hope for the salvation of ourselves and others rests in God's mercy. For the Christian, on the other side of the darkness of death, there is hope.

When Christ Cried

No matter how a loved one passes away, we all reckon with an ensuing grief and sense of loss. It's easy to lose our way in the grip of grief, but we can find hope in all circumstances because we are never left to grieve alone. Remember the story of Lazarus from a few chapters ago? We breezed through it, but I think it's worth revisiting. We know how the story ends. Jesus raises Lazarus from the dead. All ends well, but we can still learn quite a bit about grief from this story. You might recall that when Martha and Mary sent an emergency message to Jesus telling him that Lazarus was dying, Jesus waited *two days* before he began to travel to his friends. By the time he finally arrived, Lazarus was long dead.

When Jesus finally approaches their home, Martha runs to him and says what we all would say if we were in her place, "Lord, if you had been here, my brother would not have died." (Jn 11:21). It's not difficult to hear frustration in her voice. Can we blame her? Martha was friends with Jesus. She not only had heard of Jesus' healing miracles, she probably had witnessed them. She must have been wondering, "What good it is to have the Messiah as a best friend if he doesn't do for me what he has done for others?" But in the midst of her frustration and grief, Martha proclaims a bold statement of hope: "[But] even now I know that whatever you ask of God, God will give you" (Jn 11:22). Jesus then tells Martha that her brother will rise and confirms his divine power by declaring, "I am the resurrection and the life; whoever believes in me, even if he dies, will live, and everyone who lives and believes in me will never die. Do you believe this?" (Jn 11:25–26). In the midst of her grief, Jesus asks Martha to reaffirm her hope in him.

Meanwhile, as Martha spoke to Jesus, her sister Mary was at home. After hearing that Jesus had arrived, Mary approaches him. The same Mary who once sat enraptured at Jesus' feet finds herself back before her Savior, but this time overcome with grief (see Luke 10:38–42). Through tears, she repeats her sister's statement of disappointment that Jesus had not been there when Lazarus was sick. Again, we can all relate to Mary's feelings of frustration and confusion. Why doesn't God show up when we need him? Why does he sometimes delay even when someone is suffering? How can we trust God to take care of us in death? Mary is so overcome with sorrow that she weeps. Keep in mind, this is four days after her brother's death. Some might argue that she should try to pull it together; the funeral is over. But Mary doesn't hide her pain or weakness from her Savior.

Upon seeing Mary mourn, Jesus is "perturbed and deeply troubled" (Jn 11:33). Then he actually begins to weep himself. Let's not move past this profound reality. The shortest verse in the English translation of the Bible is: "Jesus wept" (Jn 11:35). Though a simple verse to memorize, it's possibly the most complex to comprehend. Jesus knows who he is and what he is about to do. This scene of grief and sorrow is about to be turned into the party of the century. Tears will turn into laughter in a matter of minutes, and yet Jesus weeps. Fully human and fully divine, Jesus experienced everything we experience but sin—even grief. He could have fast forwarded to the fairytale ending, but he didn't. He allowed himself to grieve his friend's death. He let Martha express her frustration. Mary was free to grieve. Through it all, Jesus was present, showing that his identity and love doesn't

change, even in the worst of tragedies. Martha and Mary
believed this. Do we?

Martha and Mary were not afraid to bring their grief
to Jesus and to express it honestly. Their example ensures
us that no matter how we grieve, we always can bring our
grief to Christ. We don't have to pretend we're fine when
someone dies; our grieving process doesn't have to look a
certain way. We all grieve differently. Some may be overcome by anguish, anger, or deep sadness, while others may
feel numb. American psychiatrist Elisabeth Kübler-Ross
identified five stages of grief: denial, anger, bargaining,
depression, and acceptance.[5] Often people oscillate back
and forth between them all. There's no "right" way to
grieve. Even those strong in their faith will experience a
wide spectrum of emotions while grieving. But no matter
how we mourn, in our grief, Jesus always extends grace.

Resurrecting Hope

Perhaps it sounds like a strange question, but consider
this for a moment: "What if Jesus decided *not* to raise
Lazarus from the dead?" What if he had gone and visited
Martha and Mary but never raised their brother from the
grave? Would this story still be hopeful? Obviously, Jesus
did raise Lazarus from the dead, and everyone had a happy
ending. But the reality is that hope reigned in the story not
because of the outcome but because of Jesus. In the last
chapter we looked at the reality of Jesus on the cross, but
that only covers half the story. Yes, Jesus took up his cross.
He took on the weight of our sins and paid the debt of

humanity's transgressions. The Son of God died on Good Friday. But on Easter Sunday, he rose from the dead.

Through his death and resurrection, Christ conquered his grave and every other grave. Saint Paul sums up our new reality in Christ's resurrection:

> Behold, I tell you a mystery. We shall not all fall asleep, but we will all be changed, in an instant, in the blink of an eye, at the last trumpet. For the trumpet will sound, the dead will be raised incorruptible, and we shall be changed. For that which is corruptible must clothe itself with incorruptibility, and that which is mortal must clothe itself with immortality. And when this which is corruptible clothes itself with incorruptibility and this which is mortal clothes itself with immortality, then the word that is written shall come about:
>
> "Death is swallowed up in victory.
> Where, O death, is your victory?
> Where, O death, is your sting?" (1 Cor 15:51–55)

Due to Christ's resurrection, we now have confidence in a future beyond this world. We too will experience resurrection. New life awaits everyone who puts their hope in Christ.

Jesus endured Good Friday, so we could enjoy Easter Sunday. For a follower of Christ, the resurrection means that even the absolute, worst-case-scenario can still end in union with God. In beatific bliss. For all eternity. When this profound truth is fully understood, it changes how we approach any and every tragic situation. Obviously, this doesn't mean we won't die. Lazarus was raised from the dead, but he eventually died again. Jesus never promised to save us from a physical death but from the death of our souls by sin. Hope directs us to what awaits beyond death. As Christians, we can look forward to heaven no matter what we experience in this life. Our hope is rooted in the truth that death now is merely the doorway to heaven.

Jesus' resurrection not only transformed death, but it has transformed our grief too. Of course, our hope in heaven doesn't completely alleviate our heartbreak when someone we love dies. Like Jesus, we too will weep and experience pain and loss. As Christians, however, we are called to grieve differently from the rest of the world. We grieve, yes, but we grieve in hope. One way we can grieve with hope is by praying for those who have died. Prayer for the dead is an act of hope. For, while we don't know where our loved ones are, we can hope in God's mercy that is far greater than any sin. Our prayers help the dead in purgatory—strangers and loved ones alike—to be purified in preparation to meet God in heaven. Whether or not our loved ones are in purgatory, our prayers are also a way to experience the communion of saints and the bond between all believers, living and dead. By interceding for the dead, we not only help our deceased loved ones but aid our own grieving process.

Praying for our loved ones is one way to relieve our grief and continue to love our friends and family after death. Yet, while prayer helps, no quick fix for grief exists. No magic formula or platitude can immediately fill the void a person's death leaves behind. We are not bullet-proof. Life hurts. We may be tempted to run from the hurt and pain—to bury, avoid, ignore, or numb it. But we can't avoid heartbreak. To avoid heartbreak is also to avoid the joys of life. But we can find comfort knowing that Jesus also felt grief, loss, hurt, and sadness. He does not leave us abandoned. Hope is always on the horizon. While we cherish past memories and miss our deceased loved ones, we too can look forward to the reality that with each passing day we draw closer to seeing those we love again. There is hope, even in death.

Discussion Questions

1. Have you experienced great loss in your life? If so, how did you deal with it?

2. Why can we be confident that Jesus is with us when we mourn? Have you experienced his closeness in a time of grief?

3. How would you offer hope to someone who is grieving?

CHAPTER TEN

Hope for Others

"The rich man is not one who possesses much, but who gives much."[1]

—SAINT JOHN CHRYSOSTOM

HAVE YOU EVER been to California? It's beautiful. The weather is perfect and the coastal landscape picturesque. Every time I visit the Golden State, I try to spend some time at the beach and take in a few sites. I still have several places I'd like to visit, including the Redwood State and National Park. The park is nearly forty miles of protected prairies, vast woodlands, and wild rivers. And the tallest trees on the planet are there! Thousands of years old, they can grow to have a diameter up to twenty feet and a height of well over three hundred feet. Just the trees' bark alone can be up to a foot thick. Some of these trees are so large that you could drive a truck through it—and some have tunnels carved in them so you literally can!

One might assume that such old, enormous trees would have roots that run deep into the earth to withstand winds, storms, and floods. But their roots don't run deep at all. In fact, they're pretty shallow; on average their roots are only eight feet deep. For a tree that can approach four hundred feet tall, this shouldn't be able to support a tree of that size. But, instead of running deep, the roots run wide, expanding out and away from each tree's center toward other redwoods. The trees intertwine their roots with nearby trees, interconnecting and supporting one another through the storms and many threats to their survival.

I wouldn't go so far as to say that I'm jealous of redwoods, but I admire them. And not just because they're tall and I'm short. Redwoods need one another to survive the storms of life. Their destinies are literally intertwined with one another. Unfortunately, most of us don't live like that. We struggle to rely on other people, including friends, family, and those in the Church. Attending Sunday Mass is one thing. Most of us can muster the energy to make our weekly obligation and manage a polite smile for our pew-mates. But, for many of us, developing real community in our parish, for example, can be challenging. Hope, however, is not meant to be hoarded. We are meant to become beacons of hope that light up the darkest corners of people's lives. When we are firmly planted in hope, roots of generosity will begin to grow and spread to those around us.

Generous Hope

For as long as I can remember, my parents demon-strated hope through regular acts of generosity. Sometimes they instilled in me the habit of generosity by forcing me to be generous. They'd volunteer me to babysit for family and friends. We would pick up trash on the side of high-ways. We volunteered at a soup kitchen every Christmas morning, even though I really would have rather been home playing with my new toys. Once in the second grade, while I was playing a pee-wee basketball game, I vividly remember my mom yelling at me from the stands to share the ball with my teammates. (I eventually became a decent point guard who could pass the ball to open teammates, but my jump shot is still lacking to this day. I suppose my mom deserves credit for both.) These opportunities for generosity, even if orchestrated under parental pressure, instilled in me the importance of giving.

Hope calls us to selflessness, but the world often demands selfishness. But let's be honest—life can seem much easier when we just focus on ourselves. The mere idea of looking out for ourselves *and* others can be exhausting and intimidating. When life is just about us, we reap all the benefits from our labor and efforts. And we like to think we deserve it. Why distribute what we have rightly earned or achieved? Only the strong survive in our world so we fear sharing what we have because it may put us at a disadvantage. Yet even science proves that generosity can be incredibly beneficial. Health surveys and studies have shown that generosity makes us happier.

Those who give of themselves typically have less anxiety, lower rates of depression, lower blood pressure, and reduced risks of illness[2] and cardiovascular disorders.[3] In other words, buying or taking things for oneself may grant momentary happiness but giving a gift can be profoundly rewarding. But we are not called to give just to benefit ourselves; we are called to give because it's built into our identity as Christians.

Mahatma Gandhi was one of the most influential and beloved political and social leaders in recent history. Through peaceful protests and practices, he tried to reshape and move Indian society toward harmony and equality. His work garnered him unwanted fame and recognition. Powerful and esteemed leaders and thinkers, including Albert Einstein and Martin Luther King, Jr., sang his praises. Even Pope John Paul II once visited Gandhi's grave in India to pay tribute to a man he described as distinguished by a "noble devotion to God."[4] Interestingly, while Gandhi had many Christian admirers, he never converted to Christianity. When asked why he didn't convert, though he studied the Bible and was enamored with Jesus, Gandhi is said to have responded that while he admired Jesus, he did not know any Christians who acted like him.

Gandhi points to a difficulty that many people have when presented with the Gospel message. How can others believe the Gospel message when Christians are not generous with the hope they have been given? As followers of Christ, our hope ought to push us to give freely. But what does this generous hope look like? Often the people who garner attention with their giving are wealthy philanthropists and celebrities. For instance, Bill Gates, one of the world's richest men, once gave a single gift of $4.6 billion to charity—an exorbitant amount of money, a remarkable gift![5] At the same time, Gates still sleeps comfortably knowing that he has another $90 billion or so in the bank. His donation is still meaningful, of course, but it's less impressive when you realize that it's only a small fraction of his enormous fortune.

In contrast, Jesus commends a poor widow in the Gospel of Luke for giving just a few cents to the Temple, even while other religious bigwigs were ostentatiously donating large amounts of money. Despite her small donation, Jesus commends her for putting in "more than all the rest" (Lk 21:3). In the eyes of God, generosity is not just a matter of giving, it's a matter of the heart. The question is, are we willing to give what we have?

Better to Give

In the Gospel of Mark, a young man flush with cash approaches Jesus. Not only is the man wealthy, he is also well educated and morally upright. The man knows the commandments and asks Jesus, "What must I do to inherit eternal life?" (Mk 10:17). The Gospel reveals that Jesus looked at the man, "loved him and said to him, 'You are lacking in one thing. Go, sell what you have, and give to [the] poor and you will have treasure in heaven; then come, follow me'" (Mk 10:21). Jesus looks into the man's heart and challenges him by giving an ultimatum. Basically,

Jesus is saying, "Love me or your stuff." Tragically, the rich young man chooses his stuff and walks away sad.

The rich young man had all the necessary head knowledge—but he didn't allow Jesus to have his heart. While it's easy to villainize the rich young man, are we so different? We all are protective of our belongings. After all, who doesn't like nice things? But Jesus tells both the rich young man and us that our hearts have a limited capacity. The young man's blunder teaches us that we can't fully follow Jesus if we are too preoccupied with lesser things. Acts of generosity and service not only benefit those to whom we give, but they also combat our preoccupation with the passing things of this world. The more we set our hearts on heaven, the less we are attached to earthly possessions. When we loosen our grip on worldly belongings, we can better hold onto hope.

In his Second Letter to the Corinthians, Saint Paul emphasizes the importance of self-sacrificing generosity to the early Christians. Back in those days, Corinth was a rough place to live. Think of a combination between Amsterdam and Las Vegas and you probably have a pretty close picture of what Corinth was like. Drunkenness. Debauchery. Illicit sex. Everything was on the table for the Corinthians. Nevertheless, Paul committed himself to evangelizing them and successfully won many of them over to the Gospel. After Paul left Corinth, however, some bullies came around and tried to turn the people against him.

In an attempt to win back the people to the Gospel, Paul responds to these false reports in his letters by highlighting the importance of generosity. Had I been in Paul's shoes, I don't know that I would have used the same tactic; I probably would have listed all of the dumb things they were doing and insisted they shape up. Instead, Paul brags about a little church that isn't often given the spotlight. He praises the believers in Macedonia, not because of their faith or theological expertise, but because of their generosity:

> We want you to know, brothers, of the grace of God that has been given to the churches of Macedonia, for in a severe test of affliction, the abundance of their joy and their profound poverty overflowed in a wealth of generosity on their part. For according to their means, I can testify, and beyond their means, spontaneously, they begged us insistently for the favor of taking part in the service to the holy ones, and this, not as we expected, but they gave themselves first to the Lord and to us through the will of God. (2 Cor 8:1–5)

To highlight the Corinthians' selfishness, Paul points out the Macedonians' selflessness. Though poor and afflicted, the people of Macedonia gave to Paul. If that was all they had done, they would deserve praise. But Paul points out that they even went *beyond* their means. They gave more than what was comfortable or expected. They gave until it hurt.

Paul champions the Macedonians' efforts knowing that it's something all Christians are called to emulate. Paul encourages giving because he trusts in God's abundant blessings, whether spiritual or material or both: "God is able to make every grace abundant for you, so that in all things, always having all you need, you may have an abundance for every good work" (2 Cor 9:8). Because of God's great generosity, giving leads us to the abundance of his grace. The Macedonians' example of generosity, as well as that of others, can strengthen our hope and motivate us to acts of generosity. When we focus on our own comfort and contentment, we lose the capacity to look out for others' needs. Rather than getting caught up in the rhythm of daily life and missing opportunities for generosity, the examples of generous people call us to lift our eyes from the mundane aspects of our lives and to fix our gaze on Christ.

Generous Living Is Godly Living

Back when I was in college, one snowy, winter night I went with a group of my friends into the city. As we were getting ready to head back home, a homeless man approached us. I was taken aback by the man's ragged appearance. He was only wearing a pair of old and tattered shoes, sweatpants, and a light hoodie. I was cold in my winter jacket and boots so he must have been freezing. The man asked us for money to buy food, but I didn't trust that he would spend the money on something to eat. He reeked of alcohol. I politely declined and continued on my way. As I walked away, I wondered whether I could have done something for the man. But what? I didn't have any cash on me. Even if I did, I didn't want to enable a possible addiction. I tried to convince myself the man would be OK and that there was nothing I could do. But I still felt like I had missed an opportunity.

As these thoughts flooded my mind, I realized that one of my friends was no longer wearing a coat. Without any of us noticing, my friend had run back to the homeless man to pray with him and offer words of encouragement. Then he had given the man his warm coat. Amazed at my friend's generosity, I have since reflected on that night and wondered why my thoughts and actions were so different from my friend's. I have realized that often when I am presented with opportunities to give and spread hope to those in need, doubts and suspicion inevitably arise. I question whether or not I have anything to offer, or whether I should help at all. I'm sure I'm not alone in facing this dilemma. After all, we can't help everyone; that's just a fact. And most people don't have a vast surplus of cash in their pockets. Our schedules are already full to the brim. We wonder, "What does one act of generosity really accomplish?" These thoughts and questions are natural, but too often they also become a deterrent to being generous.

Hopeful giving to those in need should not be motivated by what we can accomplish but by what God has accomplished. God is our ultimate example of generosity. After all, Jesus descended from his mighty, glorious (and probably very comfortable) throne in heaven to offer grace and redemption in the very uncomfortable, messy reality of humanity on earth. He extends his offer of grace to everyone. Not just the righteous or those he knows will be good. Not just the wayward and sinners. Jesus came for us all. He took care of our mess and wiped our slate clean. He gave his life so that we could have heaven. Our debt has been paid with Jesus' blood so that we could become the righteous, adopted heirs of the Father.

In the Gospels, we see Jesus' divine, abundant generosity time and time again. For instance, when Jesus encounters Zacchaeus in the Gospel of Luke (see Lk 19:1–10). No one in Jericho likes Zacchaeus. He's a tax collector, which means that he's also a crook and traitor to his own people. But Zacchaeus doesn't seem to care about his reputation because he's living large. One day, as Jesus is passing through town, Zacchaeus climbs a tree to catch a glimpse. To everyone's surprise, Jesus spots the tax collector above the crowd and invites himself over to Zacchaeus' house for dinner. Astounded by Jesus' generous and forgiving spirit, Zacchaeus commits his life to Christ and promises to return not only what he has stolen from the people but four times more. Jesus' act of generosity is the starting point for Zacchaeus' new way of life as a follower of Christ.

When our hearts are enraptured by the overwhelming, undeserved love of God, generosity is sure to follow. His love impels us toward others. Hope-filled living is generous living; we freely give what we have in this world as we become more captivated by the next. When we know and love a generous God, it helps us become more generous ourselves. As we emulate what God has done for us, giving our energy, time, and possessions to those in need becomes a joy and privilege.

Nearly half the people in the world live on $5.50 a day.[6] Chances are, most of us reading this book are doing better than that; we probably aren't worried about finding our next meal or a place to sleep tonight. Even if we don't have a surplus of money at our disposal, most of us have some financial resources that we can share with those less fortunate. But perhaps tithing or donating funds is not an option at the moment. That's okay. Money is not the only thing we can give. Some of us have skill sets that we can share with those in need. The math whizzes among us could offer free tutoring to needy students. The incredible athletes can teach others the skills they've learned. Even a smile or quick conversation with those who seem downtrodden can be a powerfully generous gift. While no one person is able to tackle all of the world's problems alone, each of us can make small, purposeful steps toward assisting those near us.

We shouldn't wait until we have an abundance of money, talents, or time to be generous—that day may never come. Even in times of want, we all have something to offer. No matter our circumstances, we always can offer love and be examples of faithful hope to others. When we hope, we show others what it looks like to trust God. Jesus gave us the perfect example to follow: He reached out to the marginalized and isolated. So should we. He spent time with the poor and oppressed; we are called to do the same. Jesus gave his life for others. Will we follow his example? We will become more like Christ as we imitate his generosity. Our God has been generous to us, so we have no excuse not to generously give to others. Let's not hoard the hope we've been given.

Discussion Questions

1. Think about a time when someone showed you exceptional generosity. How did it affect you?

2. Practically speaking, how does your hope in God help you to be more willing to serve and give of yourself?

3. Consider your time, money, and skills. How could you use these things to be more generous?

CHAPTER ELEVEN

Hope for Our Families

"As the family goes, so goes the nation and so goes the whole world in which we live."[1]

—SAINT JOHN PAUL II

AS I WRITE this, my children are running around the house. My two older daughters are fighting, our toddler is crying, and my son is calling for my pregnant wife to come and see what he made on the toilet. Luckily for me, but not so much for my wife, I'm on a different floor from everyone else. Most days our big, loud, spirited, energetic family is a lot of fun. Other days family life can be incredibly frustrating and almost intolerable. Maybe that's why the late comedian George Burns once said,

"Happiness is having a large, loving, caring, close-knit family in another city."

Everyone comes from a family, yet our experiences are different. Some of us are lucky and grew up in an exceptional home with loving, kind parents, a few siblings, and a friendly pet or two. Others grew up with almost the exact opposite experience of family. Some survived their parents' divorce. Some grew up without a mom or dad in the house. Others might have been foster children or were adopted and have never met a biological relative. Because of these and many other complexities that can be found within our homes, family can be a difficult topic. Family life can be encouraging, discouraging, mundane, surprising, fulfilling, and baffling all at once. And though the subject of family life may be challengingly inexplicable, the reason is not. Families are made up of broken people in relationship with other broken people, so things tend to get messy.

Nonetheless, the family is the basic building block of society, a necessary and integral part of living in the world. Despite this, the importance and reverence reserved for families has dramatically diminished over the past few decades. A large percentage of people today believe that marriage is obsolete.[2] Among couples who do get married, many marriages end in divorce. And though divorce rates of Catholic couples are lower than average, divorce is still common in the Church. In 1960 most kids lived with two married parents in their first marriage. Now less than half do.[3] In that same timespan, kids living with a single mom nearly tripled, jumping from 8 percent to 23 percent.[4]

Unfortunately, these statistics tell us what we already know—the traditional family structure is undergoing drastic changes.

Whose Idea Was This?

With rapid changes around the family in our society, it can be easy to question the institution of marriage itself. Is the idea of the family merely a social construct? Is a happy home even worth fighting for or even possible? In order to understand the family, we must go back to the beginning. Before God created the family, he made light and darkness, land and sea, and everything in between. "God saw that it was good" (Gn 1:25). Then God created Adam. But there amid all the beauty, God realized something was lacking. Adam needed a companion. Let's ponder the significance of this for a moment. Adam is chilling in paradise. He probably had a beachfront property. Maybe he had a lion or a unicorn for a pet. He's unquestionably the most popular man on the planet. But, despite the beautiful scenery and wild animals, Adam's world is incomplete because he is alone.

Enter Eve. Straight from the rib of Adam, God makes him a partner who suits him much better than any beautiful landscape or exotic pet. God's first command to Adam and Eve is for them to "be fertile and multiply" (Gn 1:28). Obviously, God isn't talking about doing math here. (Even some nonbelievers would probably admit that's an awesome command from God.) In his wisdom, God created sex so that men and women could cooperate in the creation process with him. From the union between a man and a woman comes a loving bond and a miracle: a new, distinct person. Thus, a family is formed.

Since the family was designed by God, the protection and cultivation of family life are important in his plan of salvation. The Ten Commandments reveal just how much family matters to God. The first three commandments define our relationship with God, while the last seven are concerned with love of neighbor. Kicking off the last seven commandments is the fourth commandment: "Honor your father and mother"; revealing that our love of family should be second only to our love of God. Some might be tempted to think that this commandment only applies to children, but the commandment is more complex. It indeed calls us to show honor toward our parents and elders, but it also charges parents and those in authority to be mindful and diligent of their duties toward their children and dependents. While all the commandments are beneficial to the family, this commandment points in particular to the importance of a mutual exchange of love, respect, and honor within our homes and in society.

Further, Scripture reinforces the importance of the family over and over again. Proverbs tells us, "Train the young in the way they should go; even when old, they will not swerve from it" (22:6). In the psalms we hear, "Certainly sons are a gift from the LORD, the fruit of the womb, a reward. Like arrows in the hand of a warrior are the sons born in one's youth. Blessed is the man who has filled his quiver with them" (Ps 127:3–5). In the New Testament, Saint Paul continues to emphasize this critical topic:

"Children, obey your parents in everything, for this is pleasing to the Lord. Fathers, do not provoke your children, so they may not become discouraged" (Col 3:20–21). And in the First Letter to Timothy, we find the startling warning, "And whoever does not provide for relatives and especially family members has denied the faith and is worse than an unbeliever" (5:8).

You may be wondering: Why so many instructions and safeguards for the family? It is because the family is vital for human life and has great dignity and worth. Within the family we learn how to both give and receive love, and to forgive and receive mercy. Family is also the setting where we are meant to first grasp the values of honesty, humility, loyalty, and sincerity. Further, it is within our homes that we ought to learn about God, the priority of prayer, and the joys of our faith. As Pope Benedict XVI wrote, the family is "about man himself—about what he is and what it takes to be authentically human."[5] Not only does the family develop the individual, but it strengthens society as a whole. The family can even be described as a model of our trinitarian God in the world. Saint John Paul II taught, "Christian families exist to form *a communion of persons in love* . . . living representations in human history of the eternal loving communion of the Three Persons of the Most Holy Trinity."[6] The family exists to be an image of God himself: a community of love. From the very beginning, this was God's plan for the family.

This vision for the family may seem unrealistic to some of us in the face of human realities. After all, how often do we look at the relationships in our own homes and think of the Trinity? Frequently, our families fall short of the ideal. Managing other relationships can be easier. If things go sideways with friends and colleagues, it's time to make new friends. Not happy with our boyfriend or girl-friend? Don't see a future with this person? Plenty of fish in the sea; it's time to move on. But we can't pick and choose our family. We are born into it. So how do we respond when our families seem broken beyond repair? How do we establish a community of love in our homes? How do we foster healthy relationships under our own roofs? As many of us know all too well, answering these questions can be difficult.

Far from Ideal

I once gave a talk on God's purpose and plan for the family at a conference in Wisconsin. As I wrapped up, I extended an invitation to the crowd to continue the con-versation with me after the presentation if they had any unanswered questions. After we closed in prayer, most of the group politely shuffled past as they made their way to the next lecture. Pleasantries and compliments were gra-ciously tossed my way, but no one seemed interested in a follow-up discussion. Then, looking a bit uncomfortable, a young man sheepishly approached me. His eyes were still lowered and refused to meet mine as he motioned for me to join him in the corner of the room.

The moment we were away from the other people still lingering in the room, the young man informed me that he *really* didn't appreciate my talk. He didn't mince words when sharing his displeasure. He said my teaching on the family just didn't mesh with his experience. His parents were divorced; addiction and abuse ran rampant among his siblings, and he was no longer on speaking terms with some of his relatives. He shared with me that he didn't believe things would get better, and he wasn't even sure he wanted them to improve. He had lost all hope. I listened as the young man unloaded his frustrations and struggles. He wasn't interested in my prayers or my encouragement. He came to the talk looking for a quick fix for his failing family and was disappointed not to find one.

That young man's experience of a shattered family is not unique. Save for the Holy Family, every family falls short of the ideal in our sinful world. Though families are part of God's plan, they have been broken from the start. Remember the first family, Adam and Eve? After they succumbed to the devil's temptations, Eden's power couple found themselves in sin, and God expelled them from the Garden of Eden. Sometime later, Adam and Eve had two sons: Cain and Abel. Cain, however, got jealous of Abel and ended up murdering him (see Gn 4:1–18). Think about that. One family on the planet. Four people. And they are killing each other. The dysfunction and sins of family life continue throughout Scripture. Due to their struggle with infertility, Sarah brings in a servant to sleep with her husband, Abraham, to produce an heir, despite God's promise to provide them with a son (see Gn 16:1–4). Abraham's nephew, Lot, is seduced by his daughters while he is drunk (see Gn 19:30–36). When Isaac and Rebecca's twin sons, Jacob and Esau, are ensnarled in a nasty feud, Rebecca encourages Isaac to deceive his father (see Gn 27:1–13). All of this and more happens in just the very first book of the Bible!

Many of these people are heroes of the faith, and yet their families were also neck-deep in dysfunction. Some of us may now be wondering, "If these central figures of the Bible couldn't have a perfect family, what chance does my family have? Is there hope for us?" Luckily, Saint John Paul II gave us an excellent ideal for which to strive in family life:

> There is no family that does not know how selfishness, discord, tension and conflict violently attack and at times mortally wound its own communion: hence there arise the many and varied forms of division in family life. But, at the same time, every family is called by the God of peace to have the joyous and renewing experience of "reconciliation," that is, communion reestablished, unity restored.[7]

While some of our greatest memories may be associated with our families, some of our worst pain can come from the same people. When our siblings, parents, or children make us want to scream and rip our hair out, we are called by the God of peace to foster joy and reconciliation. Though it can be challenging, reconciliation in the face of conflict is the goal toward which a healthy family strives.

The work of reconciliation in our families takes time and can require outside help. In cases of neglect or abuse, some of us may require the help of a professional in order to discern whether efforts toward reconciliation with our family members is possible or advisable. In dysfunctional and abusive family situations, it can be unhealthy and damaging to remain in close contact. When setting healthy boundaries is not possible, sometimes the best way to love our family members is from a distance. In these difficult situations, we remain hopeful, not because our relationships are necessarily going to improve, but because we know that God will continue to use everything in our lives for our good.

Back to Basics

Problems in families can be complex. But we don't need to overcomplicate our own role and responsibility within the home. The First Letter of Saint Peter reminds us, "Above all, let your love for one another be intense, because love covers a multitude of sins" (4:8). Regardless of the current state of our families, hope can direct our gaze towards the origin of all love—God who is love itself. When we are filled with God's selfless, infinite love, it overflows to our family members. As we love, we will witness a change in ourselves and our families, and our hope in God will surge. We will never be a part of a perfect family, but we can strive to be a part of a persevering family —one that continues to love and serve in the midst of the tensions of family life.

One practical way to cultivate peace, hope, and love in our homes is by praying for our families. Maybe some of us saw that coming. Prayer is always the answer, right? Parents are called to pray for their children. And young people are called to pray for their parents too; there is no tougher job than parenting. Further, we should also pray with one another. Frequenting the sacraments together, family Rosaries, and reading Scripture and devotionals are some ways we can pray together. Praying with others, especially family members, can be awkward at first. The divine dividends that come from family prayer, however, make it worth it. The power of prayer changes hearts more than anything else.

Another simple way to foster hope in our families is to serve them. Sometimes those closest to us get the worst of us. We can exert so much energy trying to impress the world that we forget to leave something in the tank for our loved ones. At times, it can be easier to direct our love toward strangers more than our own family. Full disclaimer: I struggle with serving my family just as much as the next person. Give me a chance to take a mission trip that serves the poor and needy in a third world country and I'm all over it. But if my wife asks me to empty the dishwasher, I sulk all the way to the kitchen. We don't have to become the family butler, but small acts of love have huge effects within the home.

If, because of abuse or toxic situations, it becomes necessary to distance ourselves from our immediate families, we can find consolation by leaning even further into hope. With our eyes gazing toward eternity, we can be confident that we have a loving Father who loves us unconditionally. Saint Augustine encouraged believers of this truth when he wrote, "We had a father and mother on earth, that we might be born to labors and to death: but we have found other parents, God our Father, and the Church our

Mother, by whom we are born unto life eternal."[8] Whether our family situation is closer to God's intended design or very far away, we can find hope knowing that God has invited us into his heavenly family.

Family is one of God's gifts to humanity. Since family was God's idea, it must be a good one. When we find ourselves in a home filled with drama and dysfunction, it is consoling to know that God wants us to have a happy family just as badly as we do. God *is* sovereign over each and every home. He will give us strength to love our families according to his will. Let us strive, therefore, to nurture hope in our families so that we can answer God's call to build his kingdom and to mirror his love to the world.

Discussion Questions

1. What is your fondest family memory? Your most difficult?

2. When life becomes difficult, do you find hope and comfort in your family? Why or why not?

3. What is one thing you could do this week to share God's hope with your family?

CHAPTER TWELVE

Hope for the Church

"We do not want . . . a Church that will move with the world. We want a Church that will move the world."[1]
—G. K. CHESTERTON

WHETHER IT BE across town or the country, moving is an exhausting task. The heavy lifting isn't fun, but I also loathe having to reestablish myself in a new area. Finding service providers, stores, and doctors is a tedious chore I try to put off as long as possible. When I moved to Texas, I dragged my feet before finding a dentist. Eventually, I caved and made an appointment for the closest dentistry office. When I arrived, it wasn't what I had pictured. Located in an old strip mall, the storefront was dark and grim. Inside wasn't much better. The space was as stale as the muffled music that played through the antique speakers in the ceiling. When they called me for my teeth cleaning, the experience only got worse. The gruff dental hygienist didn't make small talk, and a musty smell lingered in the air. No dentist visit can really be classified as fun, but this one was exceptionally bad.

When the dentist finally came into the room, he informed me that I had a cavity. He then said he could fix it quickly, right then and there, and wouldn't even need to numb my mouth. Though nervous, I figured it would be better to get it over with. It wasn't until after he filled the cavity that he told me my insurance didn't cover the procedure and that I had to pay the bill before leaving. A few months later while visiting my wife's family, I began chatting with her cousin. He's a dentist, so I told him about my latest appointment and the cavity. He insisted that I would have needed a local anesthetic for a filling. By the end of the conversation, he and I were both pretty confident that either the dentist was incompetent or I had been scammed.

This may seem like a strange beginning to a chapter that delves into the topic of Church. For some, the correlation between my shady dentist and their experience of Church is all too familiar. Maybe some of us have been let down by members of the Church; what we experienced didn't line up with what we expected. Some of us may have been deterred from participating fully in a parish or may even have left over the poor quality of music, community life, or the priest's homilies. Others have left the Church for much more grievous reasons. Some priests and other adults in the Church have violated trust and made evil decisions whose harmful effects have rippled through friendships, families, and congregations. Sadly, many of us are all too familiar with this. We may know both culprits and victims of heinous crimes committed within the Church.

While we can't ignore the imperfections and awful things that have occurred within our Church, it also doesn't give us an excuse to give up on the Church entirely. Obviously, my experience at the dentist is not a direct parallel to the pain or trauma some have experienced within the Church. But speaking analogously, I didn't give up on dental hygiene because of a bad dentist. Just so, it would be even more woeful to give up on the Church and everything it encompasses and offers due to the Church's members' imperfections and mistakes. Though messy and broken at times, within the Church we find a home in Christ. So if we are looking for hope, we need to look within the Church.

The Church Today

What would you think if I told you there was something you could do to live longer? What if this same thing promised to make you happier and expand your social circles? Further, what if it could grant more purpose to your life? And what if it only took sixty minutes a week? Well, guess what? According to scientific studies, regular church attendance can do just that.[2] Unfortunately, in recent years the number of people who say they believe in God, pray consistently, and participate in religious services has declined. According to one study, less than 40 percent of Catholics in the United States attend church regularly.[3] This trend impacts all Christian denominations, but the declining numbers of Catholics are staggering. Currently, the Catholic Church in the United States is losing six practicing members for every one convert that comes into the Church at Easter.[4]

As more and more people forego religious practices, a new demographic has arisen, commonly known as "nones." Not to be confused with nuns—holy women who devote their lives to Christ in the cloistered life—"nones" are a group of people without affiliation to any church, denomination, or religion. Their numbers have been steadily rising. Since 1991, their number has increased to an incredible 266 percent.[5] According to one study 23.1 percent of people in the United States now claim no religion. Today, "nones" are now more common than both Catholics and Evangelical Protestants.[6]

Though statistics can feel cold and anemic, these feel personal to many of us. For me, they represent many of my friends, classmates, and family members who have walked away from Catholicism. Some jumped over to other Christian denominations. Others left Christianity entirely for Judaism or another religion. Still others gave up their faith entirely. While a few of these people walked away due to deep hurt or frustration, most left because they were seeking fulfillment that they believed could not be found in the Catholic Church.

I'll be the first to admit that, at first glance, it can be hard to recognize the benefit of going to Mass each Sunday when the music is off-key, the homily dry, and the parking lot traffic atrocious. It's easy to wonder: "Why go to church when we can download sermons and spiritual podcasts from the comfort of our own homes?" or "Why listen to a pitchy choir when we can play our favorite worship songs from our phones?" or "Why sit with a bunch of holier-than-thou-hypocrites when we can stay in our pajamas and have a quiet moment with God in our own beds?" For the modern person, these questions are not unusual and can easily lead to the idea that the Church has become obsolete.

Father of the Church and third-century martyr, Saint Cyprian of Carthage, has a forceful reply to these notions, "He can no longer have God for his Father, who has not the Church for his mother."[7] The saint understood what many today have forgotten: the Church was founded by Christ to sustain and guide a community of believers. Knowing that we would not be able to live out the faith alone, God established the Church. Our relationship with God is meant to be cultivated through communal worship. And as we come into deeper communion with God, we find deeper unity with our fellow believers. So no matter how great a podcast or sermon on our phone may be, it can never replace Church. Just as no tone-deaf choir or dull homily can nullify the grace and life found in the sacramental life of the Body of Christ.

Of course, many people live moral, upright lives apart from organized religion and faith. I know many people who love Jesus with their whole hearts but do not like his Church. But to love Jesus is to love the Church. To separate ourselves from the Church is to separate ourselves from Jesus because the Church *is* the Body of Christ on earth. Through our Baptism, we became members of Christ's mystical body: the meaning of which extends far beyond church buildings. Because of this, all baptized people are members of the Church. We are more vibrant members, however, to the degree we participate in the Body of Christ. Like a flower uprooted from the ground, a Christian withers apart from Church.

Thus, the Church Jesus founded is far more than a social club. Rather, its purpose is to usher in his kingdom and to be a sign of hope for all. Therefore, though the communal and physiological perks of church participation are great, they are secondary to the spiritual benefits. The popularity of the Church may ebb and flow, but the grace of the sacraments has been consistently available to anyone willing to walk through the Church's doors for over two thousand years. It is within his Church that God gives himself to us in the most profound way.

The Source of Hope

When I was a college student, I had a chance to serve on a mission trip to Lourdes, France, the location where the Blessed Mother appeared to Saint Bernadette. Countless miracles have occurred at the springs of water where Mary appeared, and thousands of believers make pilgrimages to the holy site each year. For my week of service, I was given various tasks to assist with each day: I helped pilgrims enter the *piscines*, or small pools, filled with Lourdes water; I assisted the sick and elderly exit trains that rolled into the local station; and I bussed tables in the cafeterias. Though each assignment held its blessings and challenges, one task turned out to be surprisingly significant.

One day I was asked to assist during Mass. The liturgy was celebrated in the Basilica of Saint Pius X, an unusual church building. The basilica is primarily underground and *very* large. To accommodate the multitudes of pilgrims, the church is well over two football fields long and can comfortably seat twenty-four thousand people. My sole task was to assist with the distribution of Communion. I was to lead a minister of the Eucharist to his designated spot, and when the minister distributed Communion, I would hold a closed umbrella high so Mass-goers could find the Communion station. Basically, I was the liturgical equivalent of one of those people who advertise a nearby store by standing on the side of the road, spinning an arrow-shaped sign.

Though the duty seemed reasonably simple, I was unprepared for what was about to happen. During Communion, when I lifted the umbrella over my head, I was suddenly surrounded by pilgrims. In front of me, behind me, beside me: people were pressing in and reaching toward the Eucharist. I get a little claustrophobic in tight spaces, and things began to feel uncomfortable. I felt like I was being smothered. In their attempts to receive Communion, frail, older people in wheelchairs were pushing me out of the way. To be honest, I was tempted to push back. But ultimately, I was too stunned by the desire and urgency of the people rushing to the Eucharist.

After the Mass, I asked a priest what he thought about what had happened. I'll never forget his response, "Kris, when Jesus is all you have, you realize he's all you need." In Lourdes, I saw men and women who genuinely longed for Jesus with conviction and determination. Their enthusiasm for the Eucharist, however, looks vastly different from what most Catholics often experience every Sunday. When I look around on an average Sunday at my home parish, it seems as if most people, myself included, are simply on autopilot. Many seem to attend Mass out of obligation and routine rather than out of love or desire.

If we truly understood what we have in the Eucharist, more Masses would look like the one I experienced in Lourdes. The average attitude toward the Eucharist might not be as urgent and passionate as the pilgrims' in Lourdes for many reasons. One recent study gives a profound insight into why this may be the case. According to a survey by Pew Research, 69 percent of Catholics believe the Eucharist is merely a symbol.[8] But the Eucharist is not a symbol. It's not a pious ritual intended to remind us of what Jesus once did. The Church has always taught that, through the power of the Holy Spirit, what was once bread and wine becomes Jesus' Body, Blood, Soul, and Divinity.

If we long for something to buoy our hope, we need look no further than the Eucharist. The *Catechism of the Catholic Church* teaches that the Eucharist is "the source and summit" of our faith (1324). Everything flows from and back into the Eucharist, who is Jesus himself. For this reason, the Eucharist is the *very source of our hope*. In his encyclical, *Ecclesia de Eucharistia*, Saint Pope John Paul II reaffirms the connection between the Eucharist and hope:

> Those who feed on Christ in the Eucharist need not wait until the hereafter to receive eternal life: *they already possess it on earth*, as the first-fruits of a future fullness which will embrace man in his totality.[9]

The greatest peace, joy, grace, and love to be experienced this side of heaven is present to us in the Mass. In the Eucharist, we find everything we could ever want or need. He is truly present and waiting for us. When we cannot muster an ounce of hope for the future, we can turn to Christ in the Eucharist.

As Catholics, we have the opportunity and the blessing available to us to receive Jesus *daily*. The Eucharist is an incomprehensible gift of God's love and commitment to his people. This profound teaching of the Church can be difficult to grasp, but he is always available and waiting to encounter us in the Blessed Sacrament. If we ever feel tempted to leave the Church, the Eucharist is the primary reason we should remain. If we want hope, we need to stay connected to the Blessed Sacrament and Christ's Church. The Church offers both the guidance and the spiritual food necessary for our spiritual journey ahead—which also means there's more to Church than just showing up on Sunday.

Beyond the Pew

Being fully present and active in a local Church community is an essential aspect of being a part of the Church. As a member of your local parish, you can find community, accountability, catechetical programs, and Bible studies. But most importantly, in the Church we find the sacraments to assist in our spiritual growth. As the *Catechism of the Catholic Church* teaches, "The Church is the Body of Christ. Through the Spirit and his action in the sacraments, above all the Eucharist, Christ, who once was dead and is now risen, establishes the community of believers as his own Body" (805). But we must also recognize that the Church isn't just about programs and liturgy.

The word Church comes from the Greek word, *ekklesia*, or "those called out." Jesus instituted the Church through his words and actions, and he now invites us to continue what he started. The Church was never meant to be some kind of bunker for believers, a haven from pagans, hedonists, and nonbelievers. Instead, it's more like a spiritual pitstop. It's a place we pull into, get refueled, and receive the necessary maintenance so that we can speed back out into the world with grace, love, and hope for all we meet. In fact, the Church exists for its nonmembers just as much as its active members. Jesus' parting words to his disciples in the Gospel of Matthew reveal his desire for the Church:

> All power in heaven and on earth has been given to me. Go, therefore, and make disciples of all nations, baptizing them in the name of the Father, and of the Son, and

of the Holy Spirit, teaching them to observe all that I have commanded you. And behold, I am with you always, until the end of the age. (28:18–20)

This passage is called the "Great Commission," not the "great suggestion or opinion." Jesus commands his followers to "go . . . and make disciples." As members of the Church, we are called to share the Gospel with the world. We are not commissioned to sit inside a comfortable church building, but to be a grace-filled presence to others, to love, to be a sign of hope. When we live and share our faith in our homes, schools, and places of work, we are the Body of Christ active in the world. So we are not just called to go to church, but to be the Church.

Our world is starving for hope, and Jesus offers the solution for any and every difficulty we might face in this life. Once we come to know Jesus, the best thing we can do is share him with others—to evangelize. Understanding this reality, Peter instructed the early Church, "Always be ready to give an explanation to anyone who asks you for a reason for your hope, but do it with gentleness and reverence" (1 Pt 3:15–16). The genius of Peter's approach is that he doesn't urge us to get on a soapbox or start listing all the theological knowledge we have obtained. He tells us to share our hope. After all, a person can always argue with our theological or philosophical beliefs, but no one can dispute our personal and authentic encounters with Jesus Christ.

Maybe some of us have already started to list the reasons why we think this is a bad idea. Some of us might think we don't know enough about Catholicism and that we could easily say the wrong thing if someone asks a question. Maybe some of us are afraid it will be awkward or that we'd get rejected. These are all valid concerns and obstacles to evangelization, but none of them should stop us from the task at hand. We don't hesitate to share our favorite movies, songs, or books with others. Sharing our hope in Jesus is far more important. How can we withhold the hope we've found in the Church when others are desperate for it?

No formula for evangelization exists that will work for every individual in every situation. No canned speech will move every person's heart. A few foundational pieces of advice, however, can give us our footing. First, evangelization, like hope, should always start and end with Jesus. We don't need to impress someone with heavy theology or highlight our old sins for dramatic effect; we simply need to share Jesus and what he has done in our lives. Second, we must be willing to listen and allow others to voice concerns, questions, and any hesitancies concerning the faith. Dialogue always goes further than arguments. Lastly, we can trust that God will do the heavy lifting of evangelization. We already have a Savior, and we aren't him. Our job is to simply share what he has done for us and to give God the space to move.

Christ left his perfect Church in the hands of imperfect people. Even when the sins of Church members scandalize, we must remember that Jesus is the one who established the Church. He will never abandon us and is always present within the Body of Christ, even when difficult to see. We may be a flawed fellowship of broken people, but we have everything we need, primarily Jesus' presence in the Eucharist. Let's not be afraid to show others who the Church is. Hope lives in the Church, and God calls us to share this Good News with the world!

Discussion Questions

1. Do you struggle with the sins of people in the Church? Church teaching? What helps you to overcome these struggles?

2. What can you do to guard against becoming lukewarm in your gratitude for the Eucharist?

3. Have you ever shared the reason for your hope with someone? What are some opportunities to share your faith in the future?

CONCLUSION

Hope for the Future

"Everything smaller than heaven bores us because only heaven is bigger than our hearts."[1]

—PETER KREEFT

I'VE RECENTLY TAKEN up jogging. Generally, people have two approaches to new physical fitness habits. They either choose to exercise to improve overall health, physique, and well-being, or they decide to sweat just enough to eat junk food and not feel too guilty about it. My motivation definitely flows from that second school of thought. I've been running more frequently and I'm happy to report: I hate it. I have yet to experience the so-called "runner's high." Running is the worst. Why would anyone run when they can walk? That's what I want to know.

A big reason I dislike running is that I always end up back just where I started. If I run around my neighborhood, I arrive back at my front door. It isn't very exciting. So to motivate myself before I run, I drive to a place where I won't get bored. The problem is that I live in a small town with very few places to go. There's a local high school track, but that's even worse than running in my neighborhood. (Running in circles should be illegal.) So I've taken up running in the local cemetery. The cemetery might seem like an unusual place to go for a jog, but know what's even stranger? I'm starting to enjoy it. Yes, I still dislike exercise. But there's something about being on holy ground, surrounded by tombs and gravestones, that puts things in perspective. As I run through the quiet cemetery, I imagine who these people once were and what their lives were like. Were they happy? What were their struggles? What made them feel alive? And lately, as I run, my thoughts have wandered to my own death.

Our inevitable death isn't something most people like to think about, so we don't usually openly discuss the topic. But we should. Last I checked, the mortality rate for humans was still somewhere around 100 percent. Eventually, our time in this world will be over. Like it or not, death is inescapable. This reality can provoke many emotions. Wonder. Unease. Fear. We may question when and how our death will occur. We ponder what it will be like and what is on the other side of death. Thankfully, however, our hope in Jesus can ease our uneasiness about death.

Saint Peter's letter to the early Church points to the reason for hope, even in the face of death: "Blessed be the

God and Father of our Lord Jesus Christ, who in his great mercy gave us a new birth to a living hope through the resurrection of Jesus Christ from the dead, to an inheritance that is imperishable, undefiled, and unfading, kept in heaven for you" (1 Pt 1:3–4). Note what Peter does in this passage. He immediately directs their gaze away from the perishable, defiled, and fading goods of this world toward the promises of the next, because if there's no heaven, then there's no hope. Peter reminds the early Church that Christ has conquered the grave. Jesus rose from the dead and promised resurrection to all who place their hope in him. When we live with hope for the life yet to come, death is no longer as scary. As Saint Rose of Viterbo once said, "Live so as not to fear death. For those who live well in the world, death is not frightening but sweet and precious."[2] Death is not the end of our story. Because of Jesus Christ, death is like merely flipping a page to reach the next chapter.

When contemplating the truth of heaven, Saint Josemaría Escrivá once wrote, "In heaven . . . a great Love awaits you, with no betrayals and no deceptions. The fullness of love, the fullness of beauty and greatness, and knowledge . . . And it will never cloy: it will satiate, yet still you will want more."[3] You see, heaven is not merely an extension of the good things of this world. Any pleasure and comfort we find here is a mere shadow of what awaits us: "What eye has not seen, and ear has not heard, and what has not entered the human heart, what God has prepared for those who love him" (1 Cor 2:9). This is hope's goal, the prize in store for us. As followers of Christ, we place our hope in Jesus, knowing that for us he has opened the gates of heaven, where there will be no more mourning, sorrow, or pain (see Rev 21:4).

Heaven will be exponentially better than our wildest dreams. The *Catechism of the Catholic Church* teaches that heaven is the "ultimate end and fulfillment of the deepest human longings, the state of supreme, definitive happiness" (1024). Every desire and yearning within us will be satisfied, every hurt and wound healed and purified. Ironically, in heaven, the one thing we won't have is the virtue of hope. The virtue is realized and completed in eternal life with Christ. All that heaven entails will be fantastic, but what will make heaven heavenly is God. Heaven is complete and utter perfection because we will be in perfect relationship with God. Eternity is less about being in a good place and all about being in God's presence.

When we see heaven in this light, death becomes much less frightening and heaven more exciting. In *The Voyage of the Dawn Treader*, C. S. Lewis gives us a perfect example of how hopeful excitement for heaven looks. In the book, a talkative rat named Reepicheep has an unquenchable yearning to reach Narnia's version of heaven, Aslan's country. Reepicheep is on a voyage, filled with perils from enemies and the sea itself. But no matter how bleak things seem, his hope doesn't yield. At one point, he boldly declares that he will sail east toward Aslan's country for as long as he can. Even if his ship sinks, he plans to swim until he drowns with his "nose to the sunrise."[4] Even death would not drown his hope. At the end of the story, Reepicheep finally gains entrance into Aslan's country. As he approaches his final destination, his boat floats through an array of lilies, and Reepicheep trembles with delight. His journey had finally come to an end. C. S. Lewis would later tell his children in one of his letters that we should all be like Reepicheep in our pursuit of heaven.[5]

As we near the end of this book, ideally, we understand more clearly just how desperately we need hope. Hope sustains us through the suffering and passing things of this world. We can't survive this world without it. Hope is for the journey. No matter what season of life we find ourselves in today, whether we are ensnared by sin, discouraged, anxious or weary, annoyed by our families, overwhelmed by the needs of others, or feeling disenfranchised from the Church—heaven awaits. No matter how we may feel now, greater things lie ahead. Everything we see, know, and experience will pass. Like Reepicheep, we one day will arrive at the shores of paradise. And, as we behold the face of God, in all his splendor and majesty, this life's pain and suffering will fade away.

Remember the story about Florence Chadwick from the first chapter? The truth is, I only shared half her story. Though her first attempt to cross the Catalina Channel ended in defeat, two months later she was back in the water. The environment was the same: fog, sharks, and icy water. But the result was very different; this time she didn't give up. Florence held the mental image of the shoreline in her mind as she swam and reached the California coast in under fourteen hours, setting a new world record. We too can reach our goal: heaven. Jesus has given us the necessary grace through our Baptism, and he will continue to sustain us through the sacraments. Don't give up. God can use today's defeats to prepare us for tomorrow's victories. And even when it feels like we can't go any further, remember the shore might be closer than we think.

As we continue on this challenging and joyful journey toward heaven, may we hold onto the anchor of hope when the storms of life rock and shake us. God is near. He will not let us down. Let us stay close to Jesus. Heaven is waiting. I hope to see you there.

Afterword

IN THE FIRST CHAPTER, I called this book a blueprint. My goal was to give insight, clarity, and instruction on how to find and maintain hope in difficult situations. However, I never could have predicted that a once-in-a-lifetime pandemic would hit our world mere months before its publication. This pandemic has exposed a harsh reality: there are some things that we will not see coming in this life. It is surreal to think how much the world has changed and how seemingly ordinary and mundane things, like shaking a stranger's hand, have become an absurd and potentially dangerous action. Our routines, expectations, and needs have all been turned upside down in a matter of weeks.

Despite all the uncertainty, questions, and ambiguity surrounding this pandemic, God hasn't changed. No ailment or perverse circumstance can alter the truth that:

God is real.
God is near.
God has not abandoned you.

He loves you and is working for your good.
Jesus' life, death, and resurrection offers you
*   a future and a hope.*

This isn't the first time the world has gone through a viral outbreak; there have been other pandemics. In the Bible, we can see plagues and illness threaten God's chosen people and followers. Many saints lived in times of significant sickness and turmoil. Yet God was with them, giving them the grace and courage to persevere. Looking back at God's constant faithfulness ought to provide us with confidence for whatever situation in which we presently find ourselves.

Obviously, this book didn't address rogue viruses or seasons of social isolation. Maybe it should have. But just because we find ourselves confronted with a completely new scenario, the blueprint has not changed. Now, perhaps more than ever, we must lean into hope.

Will we see another pandemic like this novel coronavirus in our lives? I'd like to think we won't. However, the chances are very high this won't be the last time a situation or circumstance catches us by surprise. Confusion, pain, and even death will continue beyond this current pandemic. Other crises and calamities will arise, though they may look different. Sadly, not many circumstances in this life come with a playbook. However, our hope isn't tethered to a specific strategy but to a Savior. No matter the situation, there is hope. Always.

Acknowledgments

PAULINE BOOKS & MEDIA, it has been an honor to work with you on this project. You have been the ideal partner for publishing. From our first meetings where we dreamed up this book to the final edits and rewrites, I have felt nothing but love, grace, and collaboration from your team. Your perfect blend of professional expertise and a passion for the Gospel was exactly what this first-time author needed.

The entire Pauline staff has been incredibly supportive and helpful, but I need to acknowledge Sister Theresa Aletheia Noble and Vanessa Reese specifically. Sister Aletheia, you shepherded this book so well. You pushed me and this project beyond what I believed it could be, and when I pushed back, you were endlessly patient with me. You weren't just an editor for this book, but a team-mate; I think we made a pretty gosh-darn good team. Vanessa, you helped me get this book to the finish line. Your direction, assistance, and kindness were a godsend as we dove into some of the nitty-gritty of publishing.

Father Dave Pivonka, not only did you write the foreword to this book, but you were also the first one to encourage me to write. If it wasn't for our quick, yet prodding conversation in the middle of the Pittsburgh airport, I don't know if this book would be here today. Thank you for years of steady spiritual guidance and friendship.

Chrysan Rankin, Morgan Leverenz, Shannon Keating, and Sharon Erenkrantz, you were the first people to lay eyes on the earliest drafts of this work. Though the text has gone through many rewrites and revisions from what you initially saw, your insights and analyses were paramount in the early development of the book. I hope you enjoy the finished product.

And of course, to my wife, Grace, you deserve as much credit for this book as I do. You put up with countless evenings of my sneaking away to write in the attic while you handled the kids alone. You read and reread every draft, and gave me multiple crash courses in grammar. There is no doubt in my mind that this book would still be half-finished and sitting on my desktop without your backing and care. Thank you for living this life with me. I couldn't have asked for a better companion to join me on this wild adventure.

There are so many other people who deserve recognition, but let me wrap this up with a big thanks to my parents, family, and friends who have constantly supported me over the years. I wish I could name you all, but you know who you are.

To God be the Glory.

Notes

CHAPTER 1

1. Brian Cavanaugh, *Fresh Packet of Sower's Seeds: Third Planting* (Mahwah, New Jersey: Paulist Press, 1994), 37.

2. C. M. Antony, *Saint Catherine of Siena: Her Life and Times* (London: Burns & Oates, 1916), 29.

3. Emily Dickinson, "Hope is the thing with feathers" no. 254 in *The Complete Poems of Emily Dickinson*, ed. Thomas H. Johnson, (Boston: Little, Brown and Company, 1890), 116. https://archive.org/details/in.ernet.dli.2015.185786/page/n127/mode/2up.

CHAPTER 2

1. Thomas Aquinas, *Summa Theologica*, English trans., (1274) Second Part of the Second Part, Question 19, Article 1, 1664.

2. John Paul II, *Homily of the Holy Father at the 17th World Youth Day*, June 28, 2002, http://w2.vatican.va/content/john-paul-ii/en/homilies/2002/documents/hf_jp-ii_hom_20020728_xvii-wyd.html.

3. Saint Augustine, translated by H. Browne. *Nicene and Post-Nicene Fathers, First Series*, vol. 7., ed. Philip Schaff (Buffalo, NY: Christian Literature Publishing Co., 1888) 464. https://archive.org/stream/aselectlibrary07unknuoft/aselectlibrary07unknuoft_djvu.txt (modernized).

4. Pope Francis, *Evangeli Gaudium*, November 24, 2013, paragraph 3, http://www.vatican.va/content/francesco/en/apost_exhortations/documents/papa-francesco_esortazione-ap_20131124_evangelii-gaudium.html.

Chapter 3

1. John Paul II, *Ecclesia in Europa*, June 28, 2003. http://w2.vatican.va/content/john-paul-ii/en/apost_exhortations/documents/hf_jp-ii_exh_20030628_ecclesia-in-europa.html.

2. See Michael H. Crosby, O.F.M. Cap., *Thank God Ahead of Time: The Life and Spirituality of Solanus Casey* (Cincinnati: Franciscan Media, 2009), 76.

Chapter 4

1. Sheldon Vanauken, *A Severe Mercy: A Story of Faith, Tragedy and Triumph* (New York: HarperCollins, 1980), 83.

2. Pope Francis, "General Audience: 37. To council and to instruct," November 23, 2016, http://w2.vatican.va/content/francesco/en/audiences/2016/documents/papa-francesco_20161123_udienza-generale.html.

3. *Catechism of the Catholic Church*, Second Edition, English Translation (Vatican City: Libreria Editrice Vaticana, 1997), 43, paragraph 158.

4. Mark Twain (Samuel L. Clemens), *Following the Equator, Complete* (The Project Gutenburg, 2006), Pudd'nhead Wilson's Calendar, http://www.gutenberg.org/files/2895/2895-0.txt.

Chapter 5

1. Plato, *Timeaus*, trans. by Benjamin Jowett, last updated January 15, 2013, https://www.gutenberg.org/files/1572/1572-h/1572-h.htm.

2. Robert L. Leahy, PhD, "How Big a Problem is Anxiety?" *Psychology Today*, April 30, 2008. https://www.psychologytoday.com/blog/anxiety-files/200804/how-big-problem-is-anxiety.

3. "An Act of Hope," *Queen of Apostles Prayer Book* (Boston: Pauline Books & Media, 2014), 4.

CHAPTER 6

1. Trans., J. G. Pilkington, *Nicene and Post-Nicene Fathers of the Christian Church*, vol. 1, ed. Philip Schaff (Buffalo: The Christian Literature Company, 1886), Saint Augustine, *Confessions*, Book 1, chapter 1, 45, https://archive.org/details/aselectlibraryof01unknuoft/page/42.

2. Peter Moore, "Two-fifths of Americans are tired most of the week," *YouGov*, June 2, 2015, https://today.yougov.com/topics/lifestyle/articles-reports/2015/06/02/sleep-and-dreams.

3. Sonny Kleinfield, *Talking Straight* (New York: Bantam, 1989), 36.

4. Josef Pieper, *Leisure: the Basis of Culture*, (Ignatius Press: San Francisco, 2009), 70.

5. Thomas Aquinas, *Summa Theologica*, question 129, article 6, page 2315. https://archive.org/details/SummaTheologicaThomasAquinas/page/n83.

6. Josef Pieper, *On Hope* (San Francisco: Ignatius Press, 1986), 16.

CHAPTER 7

1. Department of Psychiatry and Behavioral Medicine, Medical College of Wisconsin, "Cue-induced cocaine craving: neuroanatomical specificity for drug users and drug stimuli,"*U.S. National Library of Medicine*, accessed January 12, 2020, https://www.ncbi.nlm.nih.gov/pubmed/11058476/0.

2. Jena Hilliard, "Social Media Addiction," Addiction Center, last edited December 6, 2019, https://www.addictioncenter.com/drugs/social-media-addiction/.

3. Christina Gregory, Ph.D., "Internet Addiction Disorder," PsyCom, last updated May 22, 2019, https://www.psycom.net/iadcriteria.html.

4. Christine Wang, "Apparently the average person takes 25,000 selfies in a lifetime. Seems about right," March 29, 2017, https://mashable.com/2017/03/29/samsung-selfie/.

CHAPTER 8

1. Saint Thérèse de Lisieux, *The Story of a Soul (L'Histoire d'une Ame): The Autobiography of St. Thérèse of Lisieux*, trans. by Thomas Taylor (London: Burns, Oates, & Washbourne LD, 1922), ch 11, https://www.gutenberg.org/files/16772/16772-8.txt.

2. James Joseph McGovern, *The Manual of the Holy Catholic Church* (Chicago: Catholic Art and Publication Office, 1906), 268, https://books.google.com/books?id=b1kWAAAAYAAJ&pg=PA268&dq.

3. Viktor Frankl, *Man's Search for Meaning* (Boston: Beacon Press, 2006), 113.

4. A Member of the Order of Mercy, *A Year With the Saints*, English translation (Hartford: The Sisters of Mercy, 1891), 136. https://archive.org/stream/AYearWithTheSaints/AYearWithTheSaints_djvu.txt.

CHAPTER 9

1. "Suicide Rising Across the US: more than a mental health concern," Centers for Disease Control and Prevention, accessed January 12, 2020, https://www.cdc.gov/vitalsigns/suicide/index.html.

2. "Suicide data,"*World Health Organization*, accessed January 9, 2020, https://www.who.int/mental_health/prevention/suicide/suicide prevent/en/.

3. Saint Thomas Aquinas, *Summa Theologica: Second Part of the Second Part*, Question 20, Article 3, 1679, https://archive.org/details/SummaTheologicaThomasAquinas.

4. Christina Gregory, Ph.D., "The Five Stages of Grief: An Examination of the Kubler-Ross Model," updated April 11, 2019, https://www.psycom.net/depression.central.grief.html.

CHAPTER 10

1. See Saint John Chrysostom, "Four Discourses, Chiefly on the Parable of the Rich Man and Lazarus (1869)", discourse 2, trans. F. Allen, B.A. London: Longmans, Green, Reader, And Dyer. 1869. http://www.tertullian.org/fathers/chrysostom_four_discourses_02_discourse2.htm.

2. See "UnitedHealthcare/VolunteerMatch Do Good Live Well Study: Reviewing the benefits of volunteering," March 2010, https://cdn.volunteermatch.org/www/about/UnitedHealthcare_VolunteerMatch_Do_Good_Live_Well_Study.pdf.

3. "Press Release: Volunteering Reduces Risk of Hypertension In Older Adults, Carnegie Mellon Research Shows," Carnegie Mellon University, June 13, 2013, https://www.cmu.edu/news/stories/archives/2013/june/june13_volunteeringhypertension.html.

4. Steven R. Weisman, "Pope Pays Tribute to India's Apostle of Nonviolence," *New York Times*, February 2, 1986, https://www.nytimes.com/1986/02/02/world/pope-pays-tribute-to-india-s-apostle-of-nonviolence.html.

5. Rupert Neate, "Bill Gates Gives 4.6bn to Charity In Biggest Donation Since 2000," The Guardian, August 15, 2017, https://www.theguardian.com/technology/2017/aug/15/bill-gates-charity-donation-microsoft-shares-foundation.

6. "Nearly Half the World Lives on Less than $5.50 a Day," *The World Bank*, October 17, 2018, https://www.worldbank.org/en/news/press-release/2018/10/17/nearly-half-the-world-lives-on-less-than-550-a-day.

CHAPTER 11

1. John Paul II, *Homily of John Paul II at Perth, Australia*, November 30, 1986, http://www.vatican.va/content/john-paul-ii/en/homilies/1986/documents/hf_jp-ii_hom_19861130_perth-australia.html.

2. "The Decline of Marriage and Rise of New Families," *Pew Research Center*, November 18, 2010, https://www.pewsocialtrends.org/2010/11/18/the-decline-of-marriage-and-rise-of-new-families/.

3. "The American Family Today," *Pew Research Center*, December 17, 2015. https://www.pewsocialtrends.org/2015/12/17/1-the-american-family-today/.

4. "The Majority of Children Live with Two Parents, Census Bureau Reports," *United States Census Bureau*, November 17, 2016, https://www.census.gov/newsroom/press-releases/2016/cb16-192.html.

5. Pope Benedict XVI, *Address of His Holiness Benedict XVI on the Occasion of Christmas Greetings to the Roman Curia*, December 21, 2012, http://www.vatican.va/content/benedict-xvi/en/speeches/2012/december/documents/hf_ben-xvi_spe_20121221_auguri-curia.html.

6. John Paul II, *Homily of His Holiness John Paul II at Ecumenical Service*, September 11, 1987, https://w2.vatican.va/content/john-paul-ii/en/homilies/1987/documents/hf_jp-ii_hom_19870911_servizio-ecumenico.html.

7. Pope John Paul II, *Familiaris Consortio*, November 22, 1981, paragraph 21, http://www.vatican.va/content/john-paul-ii/en/apost_exhortations/documents/hf_jp-ii_exh_19811122_familiaris-consortio.html.

8. Trans., R. G. MacMullen, *Nicene and Post-Nicene Fathers*, Series 1, vol. 6, ed. Phillip Schaff (Buffalo: Christian Literature Publishing Company, 1888), 281. https://archive.org/stream/aselectlibrary06unknuoft/aselectlibrary06unknuoft_djvu.txt.

CHAPTER 12

1. Joseph Pierce, *Wisdom and Innocence: A Life of G.K. Chesterton* (San Francisco: Ignatius Press, 2015), 279.

2. Duke University of Medical Center, "Does religious attendance prolong survival? A six-year follow-up study of 3,968 older adults," *U.S. National Library of Medicine*, accessed January 12, 2020, https://www.ncbi.nlm.nih.gov/pubmed/10462170.

3. Lydia Saad, "Catholics' Church Attendance Resumes Downward Slide," *Gallup*, April 9, 2018, https://news.gallup.com/poll/232226/church-attendance-among-catholics-resumes-downward-slide.aspx.

4. See "America's Changing Religious Landscape: Christians Decline Sharply as Share of Population; Unaffiliated and Other Faiths Continue to Grow," *Pew Research Center*, May 12, 2015, https://www.pewforum.org/2015/05/12/americas-changing-religious-landscape/.

5. Ryan P. Burge, "Growth and Decline in American Religion over the Last Decade," *Religion in Public*, July 9, 2019, https://religioninpublic.blog/2019/07/09/growth-and-decline-in-american-religion-over-the-last-decade/.

6. Ibid.

7. Alexander Roberts and James Donaldson, eds., *Ante-Nicene Fathers*, vol. 5, "The Treatises of Cyprian," Treatise 1, page 423. https://archive.org/stream/antenicenefather05robeuoft/antenicenefather-05robeuoft_djvu.txt.

8. "What Americans Know About Religion," *Pew Research Center*, July 23, 2019, https://www.pewforum.org/2019/07/23/what-americans-know-about-religion/.

9. Pope John Paul II, *Ecclesia de Eucharistia*, April 17, 2003, paragraph 18, http://www.vatican.va/holy_father/special_features/encyclicals/documents/hf_jp-ii_enc_20030417_ecclesia_eucharistia_en.html.

CONCLUSION

1. Peter Kreeft, *Jesus Shock* (South Bend, IN: St. Augustine's Press, 2008), 64.

2. Attributed to Saint Rose of Viterbo as her last words to her parents on her deathbed.

3. Saint Josemaría Escrivá, *The Forge*, chapter 13, number 995, http://www.escrivaworks.org/book/the_forge-point-995.htm.

4. See C. S. Lewis, *The Chronicles of Narnia: The Voyage of the Dawn Treader* (New York: Harper Collins, 1982), 524.

5. G. K. Chesterton, "The Church Congress." *The New Witness* Vol. XVIII. No. 467, October 21, 1921, p. 226. https://babel.hathitrust.org/cgi/pt?id=iau.31858045073164&view=1up&seq=650.

BOOKS & MEDIA

The Daughters of St. Paul operate book and media centers at the following addresses. Visit, call, or write the one nearest you today, or find us at www.paulinestore.org.

CALIFORNIA
3908 Sepulveda Blvd, Culver City, CA 90230   310-397-8676
3250 Middlefield Road, Menlo Park, CA 94025   650-562-7060

FLORIDA
145 S.W. 107th Avenue, Miami, FL 33174   305-559-6715

HAWAII
1143 Bishop Street, Honolulu, HI 96813   808-521-2731

ILLINOIS
172 North Michigan Avenue, Chicago, IL 60601   312-346-4228

LOUISIANA
4403 Veterans Memorial Blvd, Metairie, LA 70006   504-887-7631

MASSACHUSETTS
885 Providence Hwy, Dedham, MA 02026   781-326-5385

MISSOURI
9804 Watson Road, St. Louis, MO 63126   314-965-3512

NEW YORK
115 E. 29th Street, New York City, NY 10016   212-754-1110

SOUTH CAROLINA
243 King Street, Charleston, SC 29401   843-577-0175

VIRGINIA
1025 King Street, Alexandria, VA 22314   703-549-3806

CANADA
3022 Dufferin Street, Toronto, ON M6B 3T5   416-781-9131